Presidential Problems

CW01082915

Grover Cleveland

Alpha Editions

This edition published in 2024

ISBN 9789362095480

Design and Setting By

Alpha Editions

www.alphaedis.com

Email - info@alphaedis.com

Contents

PREFACE

In considering the propriety of publishing this book, the fact has not been overlooked that the push and activity of our people's life lead them more often to the anticipation of new happenings than to a review of events which have already become a part of the nation's history. This condition is so naturally the result of an immense development of American enterprise that it should not occasion astonishment, and perhaps should not be greatly deprecated, so long as a mad rush for wealth and individual advantage does not stifle our good citizenship nor weaken the patriotic sentiment which values the integrity of our Government and the success of its mission immeasurably above all other worldly possessions.

The belief that, notwithstanding the overweening desire among our people for personal and selfish rewards of effort, there still exists, underneath it all, a sedate and unimpaired interest in the things that illustrate the design, the traditions, and the power of our Government, has induced me to present in this volume the details of certain incidents of national administration concerning which I have the knowledge of a prominent participant.

These incidents brought as separate topics to the foreground of agitation and discussion the relations between the Chief Executive and the Senate in making appointments to office, the vindication and enforcement of the Monroe Doctrine, the protection of the soundness and integrity of our finances and currency, and the right of the general Government to overcome all obstructions to the exercise of its functions in every part of our national domain.

Those of our people whose interest in the general features of the incidents referred to was actively aroused at the time of their occurrence will perhaps find the following pages of some value for reference or as a means of more complete information.

I shall do no more in advocacy of the merits of this book than to say that as a narrative of facts it has been prepared with great care, and that I believe it to be complete and accurate in every essential detail.

GROVER CLEVELAND.
1 2 3

THE INDEPENDENCE OF THE EXECUTIVE

I

In dealing with "The Independence of the Executive," I shall refer first of all to the conditions in which the Presidency of the United States had its origin, and shall afterward relate an incident within my own experience involving the preservation and vindication of an independent function of this high office.

When our original thirteen States, actuated by "a decent respect for the opinions of mankind," presented to the world the causes which impelled them to separate from the mother country and to cast off all allegiance to the Crown of England, they gave prominence to the declaration that "the history of the present King of Great Britain is a history of repeated injuries and usurpations, all having in direct object the establishment of an absolute tyranny over these States." This was followed by an indictment containing not less than eighteen counts or accusations, all leveled at the King and the King alone. These were closed or clenched by this asseveration: "A Prince whose character is thus marked by every act which may define a tyrant is unfit to be the ruler of a free people." In this arraignment the English Parliament was barely mentioned, and then only as "others," with whom the King had conspired by "giving his assent to their act of pretended legislation," and thus giving operative force to some of the outrages which had been put upon the colonies.

It is thus apparent that in the indictment presented by the thirteen colonies they charged the King, who in this connection may properly be considered as the Chief Executive of Great Britain, with the crimes and offenses which were their justification for the following solemn and impressive decree:

> We, therefore, the Representatives of the United States of America, in General Congress assembled, appealing to the Supreme Judge of the World for the rectitude of our intentions, do, in the name and by the authority of the good People of these Colonies, solemnly publish and declare that these United Colonies are, and of right ought to be, free and independent States; that they are absolved from all allegiance to the British Crown, and that all political connection between them and the State of Great

Britain is, and ought to be, totally dissolved; and that as free and independent States they have full power to levy war, conclude peace, contract alliances, establish commerce, and do all other acts and things which independent States may of right do. And for the support of this Declaration, with a firm reliance on the protection of Divine Providence, we mutually pledge to each other our lives, our fortunes, and our sacred honor.

To this irrevocable predicament had the thirteen States or colonies been brought by their resistance to the oppressive exercise of executive power.

In these circumstances it should not surprise us to find that when, on the footing of the Declaration of Independence, the first scheme of government was adopted for the revolted States, it contained no provision for an executive officer to whom should be intrusted administrative power and duty. Those who had suffered and rebelled on account of the tyranny of an English King were evidently chary of subjecting themselves to the chance of a repetition of their woes through an abuse of the power that might necessarily devolve upon an American President.

Thus, under the Articles of Confederation, "The United States of America," without an executive head as we understand the term, came to the light; and in its charter of existence it was declared that "the articles of this Confederation shall be inviolably observed by every State, and the Union shall be perpetual."

Let us not harbor too low an opinion of the Confederation. Under its guidance and direction the war of the Revolution was fought to a successful result, and the people of the States which were parties to it became in fact free and independent. But the Articles of Confederation lacked the power to enforce the decree they contained of inviolable observance by every State; and the union, which under their sanction was to be permanent and lasting, early developed symptoms of inevitable decay.

It thus happened that within ten years after the date of the Articles of Confederation their deficiencies had become so manifest that representatives of the people were again assembled in convention to consider the situation and to devise a plan of government that would form "a more perfect union" in place of the crumbling structure which had so lately been proclaimed as perpetual.

The pressing necessity for such action cannot be more forcibly portrayed than was done by Mr. Madison when, in a letter written a short time before the convention, he declared:

Our situation is becoming every day more and more critical. No money comes into the Federal treasury; no respect is paid to the Federal authority; and people of reflection unanimously agree that the existing Confederacy is tottering to its foundation. Many individuals of weight, particularly in the Eastern district, are suspected of leaning towards monarchy. Other individuals predict a partition of the States into two or more confederacies.

It was at this time universally conceded that if success was to follow the experiment of popular government among the new States, the creation of an Executive branch invested with power and responsibility would be an absolutely essential factor. Madison, in referring to the prospective work of the convention, said:

> A national executive will also be necessary. I have scarcely ventured to form my own opinion yet, either of the manner in which it ought to be constituted, or of the authorities with which it ought to be clothed.

We know that every plan of government proposed or presented to the convention embodied in some form as a prominent feature the establishment of an effective Executive; and I think it can be safely said that no subject was submitted which proved more perplexing and troublesome. We ought not to consider this as unnatural. Many members of the convention, while obliged to confess that the fears and prejudices that refused executive power to the Confederacy had led to the most unfortunate results, were still confronted with a remnant of those fears and prejudices, and were not yet altogether free from the suspicion that the specter of monarchy might be concealed behind every suggestion of executive force. Others less timid were nevertheless tremendously embarrassed by a lack of definite and clear conviction as to the manner of creating the new office and fixing its limitations. Still another difficulty, which seems to have been all-pervading and chronic in the convention, and which obstinately fastened itself to the discussion of the subject, was the jealousy and suspicion existing between the large and small States. I am afraid, also, that an unwillingness to trust too much to the people had its influence in preventing an easy solution of the executive problem. The first proposal made in the convention that the President should be elected by the people was accompanied by an apologetic statement by the member making the suggestion that he was almost unwilling to declare the mode of selection he preferred, "being apprehensive that it might appear chimerical." Another favored the idea of popular election, but thought it "impracticable"; another was not clear that the people ought to act directly even in the choice of electors, being, as alleged, "too little informed of personal characters in large districts, and liable to deception"; and again, it was declared that "it would be as unnatural to refer the choice of a proper character for Chief Magistrate to the people as it would to refer a trial of colors to a blind man."

A plan was first adopted by the convention which provided for the selection of the President by the Congress, or, as it was then called, by the National Legislature. Various other plans were proposed, but only to be summarily rejected in favor of that which the convention had apparently irrevocably decided upon. There were, however, among the members, some who, notwithstanding the action taken, lost no opportunity to advocate, with energy and sound reasons, the substitution of a mode of electing the President more in keeping with the character of the office and the genius of a popular government. This fortunate persistence resulted in the reopening of the subject and its reference, very late in the sessions of the convention, to a committee who reported in favor of a procedure for the choice of the Executive substantially identical with that now in force; and this was adopted by the convention almost unanimously.

This imperfect review of the incidents that led up to the establishment of the office of President, and its rescue from dangers which surrounded its beginning, if not otherwise useful, ought certainly to suggest congratulatory and grateful reflections. The proposition that the selection of a President should rest entirely with the Congress, which came so near adoption, must, I think, appear to us as something absolutely startling; and we may well be surprised that it was ever favorably considered by the convention.

In the scheme of our national Government the Presidency is preëminently the people's office. Of course, all offices created by the Constitution, and all governmental agencies existing under its sanction, must be recognized, in a sense, as the offices and agencies of the people—considered either as an aggregation constituting the national body politic, or some of its divisions. When, however, I now speak of the Presidency as being preëminently the people's office, I mean that it is especially the office related to the people as individuals, in no general, local, or other combination, but standing on the firm footing of manhood and American citizenship. The Congress may enact laws; but they are inert and vain without executive impulse. The Federal courts adjudicate upon the rights of the citizen when their aid is invoked. But under the constitutional mandate that the President "shall take care that the laws be faithfully executed," every citizen, in the day or in the night, at home or abroad, is constantly within the protection and restraint of the Executive power—none so lowly as to be beneath its scrupulous care, and none so great and powerful as to be beyond its restraining force.

In view of this constant touch and the relationship thus existing between the citizen and the Executive, it would seem that these considerations alone supplied sufficient reason why his selection should rest upon the direct and independent expression of the people's choice. This reason is reinforced by the fact that inasmuch as Senators are elected by the State legislatures, Representatives in Congress by the votes of districts or States, and judges are appointed by the President, it is only in the selection of the President that the body of the American people can by any possibility act together and directly in the equipment of their national Government. Without at least this much of participation in that equipment, we could hardly expect that a ruinous discontent and revolt could be long suppressed among a people who had been promised a popular and representative government.

I do not mean to be understood as conceding that the selection of a President through electors chosen by the people of the several States, according to our present plan, perfectly meets the case as I have stated it. On the contrary, it has always seemed to me that this plan is weakened by an unfortunate infirmity. Though the people in each State are permitted to vote directly for electors, who shall give voice to the popular preference of the State in the choice of President, the voters throughout the nation may be so distributed, and the majorities given for electors in the different States may be such, that a minority of all the voters in the land can determine, and in some cases actually have determined, who the President should be. I believe a way should be devised to prevent such a result.

It seems almost ungracious, however, to find fault with our present method of electing a President when we recall the alternative from which we escaped, through the final action of the convention which framed the Constitution.

It is nevertheless a curious fact that the plan at first adopted, vesting in Congress the presidential election, was utterly inconsistent with the opinion of those most prominent in the convention, as well as of all thoughtful and patriotic Americans who watched for a happy result from its deliberations, that the corner-stone of the new Government should be a distinct division of powers and functions among the Legislative, Executive, and Judicial branches, with the independence of each amply secured. Whatever may have been the real reasons for giving the choice of the President to Congress, I am sure those which were announced in the convention do not satisfy us in this day and generation that such an arrangement would have secured either the separateness or independence of the Executive department. I am glad to believe this to be so palpable as to make it unnecessary for me to suggest other objections, which might subject me to the suspicion of questioning the wisdom or invariably safe motives of Congress in this relation. It is much more agreeable to acknowledge gratefully that a danger was avoided, and a method finally adopted for the selection of the Executive head of the Government which was undoubtedly the best within the reach of the convention.

The Constitution formed by this convention has been justly extolled by informed and liberty-loving men throughout the world. The statesman who, above all his contemporaries of the past century, was best able to pass judgment on its merits formulated an unchallenged verdict when he declared that "the American Constitution is the most wonderful work ever struck off at a given time by the brain and purpose of man."

We dwell with becoming pride upon the intellectual greatness of the men who composed the convention which created this Constitution. They were indeed great; but the happy result of their labor would not have been saved to us and to humanity if to intellectual greatness there had not been added patriotism, patience, and, last but by no means least, forbearing tact. To these traits are we especially indebted for the creation of an Executive department, limited against every possible danger of usurpation or tyranny, but, at the same time, strong and independent within its limitations.

The Constitution declares: "The executive power shall be vested in a President of the United States of America," and this is followed by a recital of the specific and distinctly declared duties with which he is charged, and the powers with which he is invested. The members of the convention were not willing, however, that the executive power which they had vested in the President should be cramped and embarrassed by any implication that a specific statement of certain granted powers and duties excluded all other executive functions; nor were they apparently willing that the claim of such exclusion should have countenance in the strict meaning which might be given to the words "executive power." Therefore we find that the Constitution supplements a recital of the specific powers and duties of the President with this impressive and conclusive additional requirement: "He shall take care that the laws be faithfully executed." This I conceive to be equivalent to a grant of all the power necessary to the performance of his duty in the faithful execution of the laws.

The form of Constitution first proposed to the convention provided that the President elect, before entering upon the duties of his office, should take an oath, simply declaring: "I will faithfully execute the office of President of the United States." To this brief and very general obligation there were added by the convention the following words: "and will to the best of my judgment and power preserve, protect, and defend the Constitution of the United States." Finally, the "Committee on Style," appointed by the convention, apparently to arrange the order of the provisions agreed upon, and to suggest the language in which they would be best expressed, reported in favor of an oath in these terms: "I will faithfully execute the office of President of the United States, and will to the best of my ability preserve, protect, and defend the Constitution of the United States"; and this form was adopted by the convention without discussion, and continues to this day as the form of obligation which binds the conscience of every incumbent of our Chief Magistracy.

It is therefore apparent that as the Constitution, in addition to its specification of especial duties and powers devolving upon the President, provides that "he shall take care that the laws be faithfully executed," and as this was evidently intended as a general devolution of power and imposition of obligation in respect to any condition that might arise relating to the execution of the laws, so it is likewise apparent that the convention was not content to rest the sworn obligation of the President solely upon his covenant to "faithfully execute the office of President of the United States," but added thereto the mandate that he should preserve, protect, and defend the Constitution, to the best of his judgment and power, or, as it was afterward expressed, to the best of his ability. Thus is our President solemnly required not only to exercise every power attached to his office, to the end that the laws may be faithfully executed, and not only to render obedience to the demands of the fundamental law and executive duty, but to exert all his official strength and authority for the preservation, protection, and defense of the Constitution.

———————————

I have thus far presented considerations which while they have to do with my topic are only preliminary to its more especial and distinct discussion. In furtherance of this discussion it now becomes necessary to quote from the Constitution the following clause found among its specification of presidential duty and authority:

> And he shall nominate, and by and with the advice of the Senate shall appoint ambassadors, other public ministers and consuls, judges of the Supreme Court, and all other officers of the United States whose appointments are not herein otherwise provided for, and which shall be established by law.

This clause was the subject of a prolonged and thorough debate in Congress which occurred in the year 1789 and during the first session of that body assembled under the new Constitution.

———————————

II

The question discussed involved distinctly and solely the independent power of the President under the Constitution to remove an officer appointed by him by and with the advice of the Senate. The discussion arose upon a bill then before the Congress, providing for the organization of the State Department, which contained a provision that the head of the department to be created should be removable from office by the President. This was opposed by a considerable number on the ground that as the Senate coöperated in the appointment, it should also be consulted in the matter of removal; it was urged by others that the power of removal in such cases was already vested in the President by the Constitution, and that the provision was therefore unnecessary; and it was also contended that the question whether the Constitution permitted such removal or not should be left untouched by legislative action, and be determined by the courts.

Those insisting upon retaining in the bill the clause permitting removal by the President alone, claimed that such legislation would remove all doubt on the subject, though they asserted that the absolute investiture of all executive power in the President, reinforced by the constitutional command that he should take care that the laws be faithfully executed, justified their position that the power already existed, especially in the absence of any adverse expression in the Constitution. They also insisted that the removal of subordinate officers was an act so executive in its character, and so intimately related to the faithful execution of the laws, that it was clearly among the President's constitutional prerogatives, and that if it was not sufficiently declared in the Constitution, the omission should be supplied by the legislation proposed.

In support of these positions it was said that the participation of the Senate in the removal of executive officers would be a dangerous step toward breaking down the partitions between the different departments of the Government which had been carefully erected, and were regarded by every statesman of that time as absolutely essential to our national existence; and stress was laid upon the unhappy condition that would arise in case a removal desired by the President should be refused by the Senate, and he thus should be left, still charged with the responsibility of the faithful execution of the laws, while deprived of the loyalty and constancy of his subordinates and assistants, who, if resentful of his efforts for their removal, would lack devotion to his work, and who, having learned to rely upon another branch of the Government for their retention, would be invited to defiant insubordination.

At the time of this discussion the proceedings of the Senate took place behind closed doors, and its debates were not published, but its determinations upon such questions as came before it were made public.

The proceedings of the other branch of the Congress, however, were open, and we are permitted through their publication to follow the very interesting discussion of the question referred to in the House of Representatives.

The membership of that body included a number of those who had been members of the Constitutional Convention, and who, fresh from its deliberations, were necessarily somewhat familiar with its purposes and intent. Mr. Madison was there, who had as much to do as any other man with the inauguration of the convention and its successful conclusion. He was not only especially prominent in its deliberations, but increased his familiarity with its pervading spirit and disposition by keeping a careful record of its proceedings. In speaking of his reasons for keeping this record he says:

> The curiosity I had felt during my researches into the history of the most distinguished confederacies, particularly those of antiquity, and the deficiency I found in the means of satisfying it, more especially in what related to the process, the principles, the reasons and the anticipations which prevailed in the formation of them, determined me to preserve as far as I could an exact account of what might pass in the convention while executing its trust, with the magnitude of which I was duly impressed, as I was by the gratification promised to future curiosity, by an authentic exhibition of the objects, the opinions and the reasonings from which a new system of government was to receive its peculiar structure and organization. Nor was I unaware of the value of such a contribution to the fund of materials for the history of a Constitution on which would be staked the happiness of a people great in its infancy and possibly the cause of liberty throughout the world.

This important debate also gains great significance from the fact that it occurred within two years after the completion of the Constitution, and before political rancor or the temptations of partizan zeal had intervened to vex our congressional counsels.

It must be conceded, I think, that all the accompanying circumstances gave tremendous weight and authority to this first legislative construction of the Constitution in the first session of the first House of Representatives, and that these circumstances fully warranted Mr. Madison's declaration during the debate:

I feel the importance of the question, and know that our decision will involve the decision of all similar cases. The decision that is at this time made will become the permanent exposition of the Constitution, and on a permanent exposition of the Constitution will depend the genius and character of the whole Government.

The discussion developed the fact that from the first a decided majority were of the opinion that the Executive should have power of independent removal, whether already derived from the Constitution or to be conferred by supplementary legislation. It will be recalled that the debate arose upon the clause in a pending bill providing that the officer therein named should "be removable by the President," and that some of the members of the House, holding that such power of removal was plainly granted to the Constitution, insisted that it would be useless and improper to assume to confer it by legislative enactment. Though a motion to strike from the bill the clause objected to had been negatived by a large majority, it was afterward proposed, in deference to the opinions of those who suggested that the House should go no further than to give a legislative construction to the Constitution in favor of executive removal, that in lieu of the words contained in the bill, indicating a grant of the power, there should be inserted a provision for a new appointment in case of a vacancy occurring in the following manner:

> Whenever the said principal officer shall be removed from office by the President of the United States, or in any other case of vacancy.

This was universally acknowledged to be a distinct and unequivocal declaration that, under the Constitution, the right of removal was conferred upon the President; and those supporting that proposition voted in favor of the change, which was adopted by a decisive majority. The bill thus completed was sent to the Senate, where, if there was opposition to it on the ground that it contained a provision in derogation of senatorial right, it did not avail; for the bill was passed by that body, though grudgingly, and, as has been disclosed, only by the vote of the Vice-President, upon an equal division of the Senate. It may not be amiss to mention, as adding significance to the concurrence of the House and the Senate in the meaning and effect of the clause pertaining to removal as embodied in this bill, that during that same session two other bills creating the Treasury Department and the War Department, containing precisely the same provision, were passed by both Houses.

I hope I shall be deemed fully justified in detailing at some length the circumstances that led up to a legislative construction of the Constitution, as authoritative as any surroundings could possibly make it, in favor of the constitutional right of the President to remove Federal officials without the participation or interference of the Senate.

This was in 1789. In 1886, ninety-seven years afterward, this question was again raised in a sharp contention between the Senate and the President. In the meantime, as was quite natural perhaps, partizanship had grown more pronounced and bitter, and it was at that particular time by no means softened by the fact that the party that had become habituated to power by twenty-four years of substantial control of the Government, was obliged, on the 4th of March, 1885, to make way in the executive office for a President elected by the opposite party. He came into office fully pledged to the letter of Civil Service reform; and passing beyond the letter of the law on that subject, he had said:

> There is a class of government positions which are not within the letter of the Civil Service statute, but which are so disconnected with the policy of an administration, that the removal therefrom of present incumbents, in my opinion, should not be made during the terms for which they were appointed, solely on partizan grounds, and for the purpose of putting in their places those who are in political accord with the appointing power.

The meaning of this statement is, that while, among the officers not affected by the Civil Service law, there are those whose duties are so related to the enforcement of the political policy of an administration that they should be in full accord with it, there are others whose duties are not so related, and who simply perform executive work; and these, though beyond the protection of Civil Service legislation, should not be removed merely for the purpose of rewarding the party friends of the President, by putting them in the positions thus made vacant. An adherence to this rule, based upon the spirit instead of the letter of Civil Service reform, I believe established a precedent, which has since operated to check wholesale removals solely for political reasons.

The declaration which I have quoted was, however, immediately followed by an important qualification, in these terms:

> But many men holding such positions have forfeited all just claim to retention, because they have used their places for party purposes, in disregard of their duty to the people; and because, instead of being decent public servants, they have proved themselves offensive partizans and unscrupulous manipulators of local party management.

These pledges were not made without a full appreciation of the difficulties and perplexities that would follow in their train. It was anticipated that party associates would expect, notwithstanding Executive pledges made in advance, that there would be a speedy and liberal distribution among them of the offices from which they had been inexorably excluded for nearly a quarter of a century. It was plainly seen that many party friends would be disappointed, that personal friends would be alienated, and that the charge of ingratitude, the most distressing and painful of all accusations, would find abundant voice. Nor were the difficulties overlooked that would sometimes accompany a consistent and just attempt to determine the cases in which incumbents in office had forfeited their claim to retention. That such cases were numerous, no one with the slightest claim to sincerity could for a moment deny.

With all these things in full view, and with an alternative of escape in sight through an evasion of pledges, it was stubbornly determined by the new Executive that the practical enforcement of the principle involved was worth all the sacrifices which were anticipated. And while it was not expected that the Senate, which was the only stronghold left to the party politically opposed to the President, would contribute an ugly dispute to a situation already sufficiently troublesome, I am in a position to say that even such a contingency, if early made manifest, would have been contemplated with all possible fortitude.

The Tenure of Office act, it will be remembered, was passed in 1867 for the express purpose of preventing removals from office by President Johnson, between whom and the Congress a quarrel at that time raged, so bitter that it was regarded by sober and thoughtful men as a national affliction, if not a scandal.

An amusing story is told of a legislator who, endeavoring to persuade a friend and colleague to aid him in the passage of a certain measure in which he was personally interested, met the remark that his bill was unconstitutional with the exclamation, "What does the Constitution amount to between friends?" It would be unseemly to suggest that in the heat of strife the majority in Congress had deliberately determined to pass an unconstitutional law, but they evidently had reached the point where they considered that what seemed to them the public interest and safety justified them, whatever the risk might be, in setting aside the congressional construction given to the Constitution seventy-eight years before.

The law passed in 1867 was exceedingly radical, and in effect distinctly purported to confer upon the Senate the power of preventing the removal of officers without the consent of that body. It was provided that during a recess of the Senate an officer might be suspended only in case it was shown by evidence satisfactory to the President, that the incumbent was guilty of misconduct in office or crime, or when for any reason he should become incapable or legally disqualified to perform his duties; and that within twenty days after the beginning of the next session of the Senate, the President should report to that body such suspension, with the evidence and reasons for his action in the case, and the name of the person designated by the President to perform temporarily the duties of the office. Then follows this provision:

> And if the Senate shall concur in such suspension and advise and consent to the removal of such officer, they shall so certify to the President, who may thereupon remove said officer, and by and with the advice and consent of the Senate appoint another person to such office. But if the Senate shall refuse to concur in such suspension, such officer so suspended shall forthwith resume the functions of his office.

On the 5th of April, 1869, a month and a day after President Johnson was succeeded in the Presidency by General Grant, that part of the act of 1867 above referred to, having answered the purpose for which it was passed, was repealed, and other legislation was enacted in its place. It was provided in the new statute that the President might "in his discretion," during the recess of that body, suspend officials until the end of the next session of the Senate, and designate suitable persons to perform the duties of such suspended officer in the meantime; and that such designated persons should be subject to removal in the discretion of the President by the designation of others. The following, in regard to the effect of such suspension, was inserted in lieu of the provision on that subject in the law of 1867 which I have quoted:

> And it shall be the duty of the President within thirty days after the commencement of each session of the Senate, except for any office which in his opinion ought not to be filled, to nominate persons to fill all vacancies in office which existed at the meeting of the Senate, whether temporarily filled or not, and also in the place of all officers suspended; and if the Senate, during such session, shall refuse to advise and consent to an appointment in the place of any suspended officer, then, and not otherwise, the President shall nominate another person as soon as practicable to said session of the Senate for said office.

This was the condition of the so-called tenure of office legislation when a Democratic President was inaugurated and placed in expected coöperation with a Republican majority in the Senate—well drilled, well organized, with partizanship enough at least to insure against indifference to party advantage, and perhaps with here and there a trace of post-election irritation.

Whatever may be said as to the constitutionality of the Tenure of Office laws of 1867 and 1869, certainly the latter statute did not seem, in outside appearance, to be charged with explosive material that endangered Executive prerogative. It grew out of a bill for the absolute and unconditional repeal of the law of 1867 relating to removals and suspensions. This bill originated in the House of Representatives, and passed that body so nearly unanimously that only sixteen votes were recorded against it. In the Senate, however, amendments were proposed, which being rejected by the House, a committee of conference was appointed to adjust, by compromise if possible, the controversy between the two bodies. This resulted in an agreement by the committee upon the provisions of the law of 1869, as a settlement of the difficulty. In the debate in the House of Representatives on the report of the committee, great uncertainty and differences of opinion were developed as to its meaning and effect. Even the House conferees differed in their explanation of it. Members were assured that the proposed modifications of the law of 1867, if adopted, would amount to its complete repeal; and it was also asserted with equal confidence that some of its objectionable limitations upon executive authority would still remain in force. In this state of confusion and doubt the House of Representatives, which a few days before had passed a measure for unconditional repeal, with only sixteen votes against it, adopted the report of the conference committee with sixty-seven votes in the negative.

So far as removals following suspensions are concerned, the language of the law of 1869 certainly seems to justify the understanding that in this particular it virtually repealed the existing statute.

The provision permitting the President to suspend only on certain specified grounds was so changed as to allow him to make such suspensions "in his discretion." The requirements that the President should report to the Senate "the evidence and reasons for his action in the case," and making the advice and consent of the Senate necessary to the removal of a suspended officer, were entirely eliminated; and in lieu of the provision in the law of 1867 that "if the Senate shall refuse to concur in such suspension, such officer so suspended shall forthwith resume the functions of his office," the law of 1869, after requiring the President to send to the Senate nominations to fill the place of officers who had been "in his discretion" suspended, declared "that if the Senate, during such session, shall refuse to advise and consent to an appointment in the place of any suspended officer,"—that is, shall refuse to confirm the person appointed by the President in place of the officer suspended,—not that "such officer so suspended shall resume the functions of his office," but that "then, and not otherwise, the President shall nominate another person as soon as practicable to said session of the Senate for said office."

It seems to me that the gist of the whole matter is contained in a comparison of these two provisions. Under the law of 1867 the incumbent is only conditionally suspended, still having the right to resume his office in case the Senate refuses to concur in the suspension; but under the law of 1869 the Senate had no concern with the suspension of the incumbent, nor with the discretion vested in the President in reference thereto by the express language of the statute; and the suspended incumbent was beyond official resuscitation. Instead of the least intimation that in any event he might "resume the functions of his office," as provided in the law of 1867, it is especially declared that in case the Senate shall refuse to advise and consent to the appointment of the particular person nominated by the President in place of the suspended official, he shall nominate another person to the Senate for such office. Thus the party suspended seems to be eliminated from consideration, the Senate is relegated to its constitutional rights of confirming or rejecting nominations as it sees fit, and the President is reinstated in his undoubted constitutional power of removal through the form of suspension.

In addition to what is apparent from a comparison of these two statutes, it may not be improper to glance at certain phases of executive and senatorial action since the passage of the law of 1869 as bearing upon the theory that, so far as it dealt with suspensions and their effect, if it did not amount to a repeal of the law of 1867, it at least extinguished all its harmful vitality as a limitation of executive prerogative. It has been stated, apparently by authority, that President Grant within seven weeks after his inauguration on the 4th of March, 1869, sent to the Senate six hundred and eighty cases of removals or suspensions, all of which I assume were entirely proper and justifiable. I cannot tell how many of the cases thus submitted to the Senate were suspensions, nor how many of them purported to be removals; nor do I know how many nominations of new officers accompanying them were confirmed. It appears that ninety-seven of them were withdrawn before they were acted upon by the Senate; and inasmuch as the law of 1867 was in force during four of the seven weeks within which these removals and suspensions were submitted, it is barely possible that these withdrawals were made during the four weeks when the law of 1867 was operative, to await a more convenient season under the law of 1869. Attention should be here called, however, to the dissatisfaction of President Grant, early in his incumbency, with the complexion of the situation, even under the repealing and amendatory law of 1869. In his first annual message to the Congress in December, 1869, he complained of that statute as "being inconsistent with a faithful and efficient administration of the Government," and recommended its repeal. Perhaps he was led to apprehend that the Senate would claim under its provisions the power to prevent the President from putting out of office an undesirable official by suspension. This is indicated by the following sentence in his message: "What faith can an Executive put in officials forced upon him, and those, too, whom he has suspended for reason?" Or it may be possible that he did not then appreciate how accommodatingly the law might be construed or enforced when the President and Senate were in political accord. However these things may be, it is important to observe, in considering the light in which the law of 1869 came to be regarded by both the Executive and the Senate, that President Grant did not deem it necessary afterward to renew his recommendation for its repeal, and that at no time since its enactment has its existence been permitted to embarrass executive action prior to the inauguration of a President politically opposed to the majority in the Senate.

The review which I have thus made of the creation of our national Executive office, and of certain events and incidents which interpreted its powers and functions, leads me now to a detailed account of the incident mentioned by me at the beginning as related to the general subject under discussion and in which I was personally concerned. But before proceeding further, I desire to say that any allusion I may have made, or may hereafter make, recognizing the existence of partizanship in certain quarters does not arise from a spirit of complaint or condemnation. I intend no more by such allusions than to explain and illustrate the matters with which I have to deal by surrounding conditions and circumstances. I fully appreciate the fact that partizanship follows party organization, that it is apt to be unduly developed in all parties, and that it often hampers the best aspirations and purposes of public life; but I hope I have reached a condition when I can recall such adverse partizanship as may have entered into past conflicts and perplexities, without misleading irritation or prejudice.

III

Immediately after the change of administration in 1885, the pressure began for the ousting of Republican office-holders and the substitution of Democrats in their places. While I claim to have earned a position which entitles me to resent the accusation that I either openly or covertly favor swift official decapitation for partizan purposes, I have no sympathy with the intolerant people who, without the least appreciation of the meaning of party work and service, superciliously affect to despise all those who apply for office as they would those guilty of a flagrant misdemeanor. It will indeed be a happy day when the ascendancy of party principles, and the attainment of wholesome administration, will be universally regarded as sufficient rewards of individual and legitimate party service. Much has already been accomplished in the direction of closing the door of partizanship as an entrance to public employment; and though this branch of effort in the public interest may well be still further extended, such extension certainly should be supplemented by earnest and persuasive attempts to correct among our people long-cherished notions concerning the ends that should be sought through political activity, and by efforts to uproot pernicious and office-rewarding political methods. I am not sure that any satisfactory progress can be made toward these results, until our good men with unanimity cease regarding politics as necessarily debasing, and by active participation shall displace the selfish and unworthy who, when uninterrupted, control party operations. In the meantime, why should we indiscriminately hate those who seek office? They may not have entirely emancipated themselves from the belief that the offices should pass with party victory; but even if this is charged against them, it can surely be said that in all other respects they are in many instances as honest, as capable, and as intelligent as any of us. There may be reasons and considerations which properly defeat their aspirations, but their applications are not always disgraceful. I have an idea that sometimes the greatest difference between them and those who needlessly abuse them and gloat over their discomfiture, consists in the fact that the office-seekers desire office, and their critics, being more profitably employed, do not. I feel constrained to say this much by way of defending, or at least excusing, many belonging to a numerous contingent of citizens, who, after the 4th of March, 1885, made large drafts upon my time, vitality, and patience; and I feel bound to say that in view of their frequent disappointments, and the difficulty they found in appreciating the validity of the reasons given for refusing their applications, they accepted the situation with as much good nature and contentment as could possibly have been anticipated. It must be remembered that they and their party associates had been banished from Federal office-holding for twenty-four years.

I have no disposition to evade the fact that suspensions of officials holding presidential commissions began promptly and were quite vigorously continued; but I confidently claim that every suspension made was with honest intent and, I believe, in accordance with the requirements of good administration and consistent with prior executive pledges. Some of these officials held by tenures unlimited as to their duration. Among these were certain internal-revenue officers who, it seemed to me, in analogy with others doing similar work but having a limited tenure, ought to consider a like limited period of incumbency their proper term of office; and there were also consular officials and others attached to the foreign service who, I believe it was then generally understood, should be politically in accord with the administration.

By far the greater number of suspensions, however, were made on account of gross and indecent partizan conduct on the part of the incumbents. The preceding presidential campaign, it will be recalled, was exceedingly bitter, and governmental officials then in place were apparently so confident of the continued supremacy of their party that some of them made no pretense of decent behavior. In numerous instances the post-offices were made headquarters for local party committees and organizations and the centers of partizan scheming. Party literature favorable to the postmasters' party, that never passed regularly through the mails, was distributed through the post-offices as an item of party service, and matter of a political character, passing through the mails in the usual course and addressed to patrons belonging to the opposite party, was withheld; disgusting and irritating placards were prominently displayed in many post-offices, and the attention of Democratic inquirers for mail matter was tauntingly directed to them by the postmaster; and in various other ways postmasters and similar officials annoyed and vexed those holding opposite political opinions, who, in common with all having business at public offices, were entitled to considerate and obliging treatment. In some quarters official incumbents neglected public duty to do political work, and especially in Southern States they frequently were not only inordinately active in questionable political work, but sought to do party service by secret and sinister manipulation of colored voters, and by other practices inviting avoidable and dangerous collisions between the white and colored population.

I mention these things in order that what I shall say later may be better understood. I by no means attempt to describe all the wrongdoing which formed the basis of many of the suspensions of officials that followed the inauguration of the new administration. I merely mention some of the accusations which I recall as having been frequently made, by way of illustrating in a general way certain phases of pernicious partizanship that seemed to me to deserve prompt and decisive treatment. Some suspensions, however, were made on proof of downright official malfeasance. Complaints against office-holders based on personal transgression or partizan misconduct were usually made to the Executive and to the heads of departments by means of letters, ordinarily personal and confidential, and also often by means of verbal communications.

Whatever papers, letters, or documents were received on the subject, either by the President or by any head of department, were, for convenience of reference, placed together on department files. These complaints were carefully examined; many were cast aside as frivolous or lacking support, while others, deemed of sufficient gravity and adequately established, resulted in the suspension of the accused officials.

Suspensions instead of immediate removals were resorted to, because under the law then existing it appeared to be the only way that during a recess of the Senate an offending official could be ousted from his office, and his successor installed pending his nomination to the Senate at its next session. Though, as we have already seen, the law permitted suspensions by the President "in his discretion," I considered myself restrained by the pledges I had made from availing myself of the discretion thus granted without reasons, and felt bound to make suspensions of officials having a definite term to serve, only for adequate cause.

It will be observed further on that no resistance was then made to the laws pertaining to executive removals and suspensions, on the ground of their unconstitutionality; but I have never believed that either the law of 1867 or the law of 1869, when construed as permitting interference with the freedom of the President in making removals, would survive a judicial test of its constitutionality.

Within thirty days after the Senate met in December, 1885, the nominations of the persons who had been designated to succeed officials suspended during the vacation were sent to that body for confirmation, pursuant to existing statutes.

It was charged against me by the leader of the majority in the Senate that these nominations of every kind and description, representing the suspensions made within ten months succeeding the 4th of March, 1885, numbered six hundred and forty-three. I have not verified this statement, but I shall assume that it is correct. Among the officials suspended there were two hundred and seventy-eight postmasters, twenty-eight district attorneys, and twenty-four marshals, and among those who held offices with no specified term there were sixty-one internal-revenue officers and sixty-five consuls and other persons attached to the foreign service.

It was stated on the floor of the Senate, after it had been in session for three months, that of the nominations submitted to that body to fill the places of suspended officials fifteen had been confirmed and two rejected.

Quite early in the session frequent requests in writing began to issue from the different committees of the Senate to which these nominations were referred, directed to the heads of the several departments having supervision of the offices to which the nominations related, asking the reasons for the suspension of officers whose places it was proposed to fill by means of the nominations submitted, and for all papers on file in their departments which showed the reasons for such suspensions. These requests foreshadowed what the senatorial construction of the law of 1869 might be, and indicated that the Senate, notwithstanding constitutional limitations, and even in the face of the repeal of the statutory provision giving it the right to pass upon suspensions by the President, was still inclined to insist, directly or indirectly, upon that right. These requests, as I have said, emanated from committees of the Senate, and were addressed to the heads of departments. As long as such requests were made by committees I had no opportunity to discuss the questions growing out of such requests with the Senate itself, or to make known directly to that body the position on this subject which I felt bound to assert. Therefore the replies made to committees by the different heads of departments stated that by direction of the President they declined furnishing the reasons and papers so requested, on the ground that the public interest would not be thereby promoted, or on the ground that such reasons and papers related to a purely executive act. Whatever language was used in these replies, they conveyed the information that the President had directed a denial of the requests made, because in his opinion the Senate could have no proper concern with the information sought to be obtained.

It may not be amiss to mention here that while this was the position assumed by the Executive in relation to suspensions, all the information of any description in the possession of the Executive or in any of the departments, which would aid in determining the character and fitness of those nominated in place of suspended officials, was cheerfully and promptly furnished to the Senate or its committees when requested.

In considering the requests made for the transmission of the reasons for suspensions, and the papers relating thereto, I could not avoid the conviction that a compliance with such requests would be to that extent a failure to protect and defend the Constitution, as well as a wrong to the great office I held in trust for the people, and which I was bound to transmit unimpaired to my successors; nor could I be unmindful of a tendency in some quarters to encroach upon executive functions, or of the eagerness with which executive concession would be seized upon as establishing precedent.

The nominations sent to the Senate remained neglected in the committees to which they had been referred; the requests of the committees for reasons and papers touching suspensions were still refused, and it became daily more apparent that a sharp contest was impending. In this condition of affairs it was plainly intimated by members of the majority in the Senate that if all charges against suspended officials were abandoned and their suspensions based entirely upon the ground that the spoils belonged to the victors, confirmations would follow. This, of course, from my standpoint, would have been untruthful and dishonest; but the suggestion indicated that in the minds of some Senators, at least, there was a determination to gain a partizan advantage by discrediting the professions of the President, who, for the time, represented the party they opposed. This manifestly could be thoroughly done by inducing him to turn his back upon the pledges he had made, and to admit, for the sake of peace, that his action arose solely from a desire to put his party friends in place.

Up to this stage of the controversy, not one of the many requests made for the reasons of suspensions or for the papers relating to them had been sent from the Senate itself; nor had any of them been addressed to the President. It may seem not only strange that, in the existing circumstances, the Senate should have so long kept in the background, but more strange that the Executive, constituting a coördinate branch of the Government, and having such exclusive concern in the pending differences, should have been so completely ignored. I cannot think it uncharitable to suggest in explanation that as long as these requests and refusals were confined to Senate committees and heads of departments, a public communication stating the position of the President in the controversy would probably be avoided; and that, as was subsequently made more apparent, there was an intent, in addressing requests to the heads of departments, to lay a foundation for the contention that not only the Senate but its committees had a right to control these heads of departments as against the President in matters relating to executive duty.

On the 17th of July, 1885, during the recess of the Senate, one George M. Duskin was suspended from the office of District Attorney for the Southern District of Alabama, and John D. Burnett was designated as his successor. The latter at once took possession of the office, and entered upon the discharge of its duties; and on the 14th of December, 1885, the Senate having in the meantime convened in regular session, the nomination of Burnett was sent to that body for confirmation. This nomination, pursuant to the rules and customs of the Senate, was referred to its Committee on the Judiciary. On the 26th of December, that committee then having the nomination under consideration, one of its members addressed a communication to the Attorney-General of the United States, requesting him, "on behalf of the Committee on the Judiciary of the Senate and by its direction," to send to such member of the committee all papers and information in the possession of the Department of Justice touching the nomination of Burnett, "also all papers and information touching the suspension and proposed removal from office of George M.

Duskin." On the 11th of January, 1886, the Attorney-General responded to this request in these terms:

> The Attorney-General states that he sends herewith all papers, etc., touching the nomination referred to; and in reference to the papers touching the suspension of Duskin from office, he has as yet received no direction from the President in relation to their transmission.

At this point it seems to have been decided for the first time that the Senate itself should enter upon the scene as interrogator. It was not determined, however, to invite the President to answer this new interrogator, either for the protection and defense of his high office or in self-vindication. It appears to have been also decided at this time to give another form to the effort the Senate itself was to undertake to secure the "papers and information" which its Committee had been unable to secure. In pursuance of this plan the following resolution was adopted by the Senate in executive session on the 25th of January, 1886:

> Resolved, That the Attorney-General of the United States be, and he hereby is, directed to transmit to the Senate copies of all documents and papers that have been filed in the Department of Justice since the 1st day of January, a.d. 1885, in relation to the conduct of the office of District Attorney of the United States for the Southern District of Alabama.

The language of this resolution is more adroit than ingenuous. While appearing reasonable and fair upon its face, and presenting no indication that it in any way related to a case of suspension, it quickly assumes its real complexion when examined in the light of its surroundings. The requests previously made on behalf of Senate committees had ripened into a "demand" by the Senate itself. Herein is found support for the suggestion I have made, that from the beginning there might have been an intent on the part of the Senate to claim that the heads of departments, who are members of the President's Cabinet and his trusted associates and advisers, owed greater obedience to the Senate than to their executive chief in affairs which he and they regarded as exclusively within executive functions. As to the real meaning and purpose of the resolution, a glance at its accompanying conditions and the incidents preceding it makes manifest the insufficiency of its disguise. This resolution was adopted by the Senate in executive session, where the entire senatorial business done is the consideration of treaties and the confirmation of nominations for office. At the time of its adoption Duskin had been suspended for more than six months, his successor had for that length of time been in actual possession of the office, and this successor's nomination was then before the Senate in executive session for confirmation. The demand was for copies of documents and papers in relation to the conduct of the office filed since January 1, 1885, thus covering a period of incumbency almost equally divided between the suspended officer and the person nominated to succeed him. The documents and papers demanded could not have been of any possible use to the Senate in executive session, except as they had a bearing either upon the suspension of the one or the nomination of the other. But as we have already seen, the Attorney-General had previously sent to a committee of the Senate all the papers he had in his custody in any way relating to the nomination and the fitness of the nominee, whether such papers had reference to the conduct of the office or otherwise. Excluding, therefore, such documents and papers embraced in the demand as related to the pending nomination, and which had already been transmitted, it was plain that there was nothing left with the Attorney-General that could be included in the demand of the Senate in its executive session except what had reference to the conduct of the previous incumbent and his suspension. It is important to recall in this connection the fact that this subtle demand of the Senate for papers relating "to the conduct of the office" followed closely upon a failure to obtain "all papers and information" touching said suspension, in response to a plain and blunt request specifying precisely what was desired.

IV

I have referred to these matters because it seems to me they indicate the animus and intent which characterized the first stages of a discussion that involved the rights and functions of the Executive branch of the Government. It was perfectly apparent that the issue was between the President and the Senate, and that the question constituting that issue was whether or not the Executive was invested with the right and power to suspend officials without the interference of the Senate or any accountability to that body for the reasons of his action. It was also manifest if it was desired to deal with this issue directly and fairly, disembarrassed by any finesse for position, it could at any time have been easily done, if only one of the many requests for reasons for suspensions, which were sent by committees of the Senate to heads of departments, had been sent by the Senate itself to the President.

Within three days after the passage by the Senate, in executive session, of the resolution directing the Attorney-General to transmit to that body the documents and papers on file relating to the management and conduct of the office from which Mr. Duskin had been removed, and to which Mr.

Burnett had been nominated, the Attorney-General replied thereto as follows:

> In response to the said resolution, the President of the United States directs me to say that the papers that were in this department relating to the fitness of John D. Burnett, recently nominated to said office, having already been sent to the Senate Committee on the Judiciary, and the papers and documents which are mentioned in the said resolution, and still remaining in the custody of this department, having exclusive reference to the suspension by the President of George M. Duskin, the late incumbent of the office of District Attorney for the Southern District of Alabama, it is not considered that the public interests will be promoted by a compliance with said resolution and the transmission of the papers and documents therein mentioned to the Senate in executive session.

This response of the Attorney-General was referred to the Senate Committee on the Judiciary. Early in February, 1886, a majority of the committee made a report to the Senate, in which it seems to have been claimed that all papers—whatever may be their personal, private, or confidential character—if placed on file, or, in other words, if deposited in the office of the head of a department, became thereupon official papers, and that the Senate had therefore a right to their transmittal when they had reference to the conduct of a suspended official, and when that body had under advisement the confirmation of his proposed successor. Much stress was laid upon the professions made by the President of his adherence to Civil Service reform methods, and it was broadly hinted that, in the face of six hundred and forty-three suspensions from office, these professions could hardly be sincere. Instances were cited in which papers and information had been demanded and furnished in previous administrations, and these were claimed to be precedents in favor of the position assumed by the majority of the committee. Almost at the outset of the report it was declared:

> The important question, then, is whether it is within the constitutional competence of either House of Congress to have access to the official papers and documents in the various public offices of the United States, created by laws enacted by themselves.

In conclusion, the majority recommended the adoption by the Senate of the following resolutions:

Resolved, That the Senate hereby expresses its condemnation of the refusal of the Attorney-General, under whatever influence, to send to the Senate copies of papers called for by its resolution of the 25th of January and set forth in the report of the Committee on the Judiciary, as in violation of his official duty and subversive of the fundamental principles of the Government, and of a good administration thereof.

Resolved, That it is under these circumstances the duty of the Senate to refuse its advice and consent to proposed removals of officers, the documents and papers in reference to the supposed official or personal misconduct of whom are withheld by the Executive or any head of a department when deemed necessary by the Senate and called for in considering the matter.

Resolved, That the provision of Section 1754 of the Revised Statutes, declaring that persons honorably discharged from the military or naval service by reason of disability resulting from wounds or sickness incurred in the line of duty shall be preferred for appointment to civil offices provided they are found to possess the business capacity necessary for the proper discharge of the duties of such offices, ought to be faithfully and fully put in execution, and that to remove or to propose to remove any such soldier whose faithfulness, competency, and character are above reproach, and to give place to another who has not rendered such service, is a violation of the spirit of the law and of the practical gratitude the people and the Government of the United States owe to the defenders of constitutional liberty and the integrity of the Government.

The first of these resolutions contains charges which, if true, should clearly furnish grounds for the impeachment of the Attorney-General—if not the President under whose "influence" he concededly refused to submit the papers demanded by the Senate. A public officer whose acts are "in violation of his official duty and subversive of the fundamental principles of the Government, and of a good administration thereof," can scarcely add anything to his predicament of guilt.

The second resolution has the merit of honesty in confessing that the intent and object of the demand upon the Attorney-General was to secure the demanded papers and documents for the purpose of passing upon the

President's reasons for suspension. Beyond this, the declaration it contains, that it was the "duty of the Senate to refuse its advice and consent to proposed removals of officers" when the papers and documents relating to their "supposed official or personal misconduct" were withheld, certainly obliged the Senate, if the resolution should be adopted, and if the good faith of that body in the controversy should be assumed, to reject or ignore all nominations made to succeed suspended officers unless the documents and papers upon which the suspension was based were furnished and the Senate was thus given an opportunity to review and reverse or confirm the President's executive act, resting, by the very terms of existing law, "in his discretion."

The third resolution is grandly phrased, and its sentiment is patriotic, noble, and inspiriting. Inasmuch, however, as the removal of veteran soldiers from office did not seem to assume any considerable prominence in the arraignment of the administration, the object of the resolution is slightly obscure, unless, as was not unusual in those days, the cause of the old soldier was impressed into the service of the controversy for purposes of general utility.

A minority report was subsequently submitted, signed by all the Democratic members of the committee, in which the allegations of the majority report were sharply controverted. It was therein positively asserted that no instance could be found in the practice of the Government whose similarity in its essential features entitled it to citation as an authoritative precedent; and that neither the Constitution nor the existing law afforded any justification for the action of the Senate in the promises.

These two reports, of course, furnished abundant points of controversy. About the time of their submission, moreover, another document was addressed to the Senate, which, whatever else may be said of it, seems to have contributed considerably to the spirit and animation of the discussion that ensued. This was a message from the President, in which his position concerning the matter in dispute was defined. In this communication the complete and absolute responsibility of the President for all suspensions and the fact that the Executive had been afforded no opportunity to speak for himself was stated in the following terms:

> Though these suspensions are my executive acts based upon considerations addressed to me alone, and for which I am wholly responsible, I have had no invitation from the Senate to state the position which I have felt constrained to assume in relation to the same, or to interpret for myself my acts and motives in the premises. In this condition of affairs I have forborne addressing the Senate

upon the subject, lest I might be accused of thrusting myself unbidden upon the attention of that body.

This statement was accompanied by the expression of a hope that the misapprehension of the Executive position, indicated in the majority report just presented and published, might excuse his then submitting a communication. He commented upon the statement in the report that "the important question, then, is whether it is within the constitutional competence of either House of Congress to have access to the official papers and documents in the various public offices of the United States, created by laws enacted by themselves," by suggesting that though public officials of the United States might be created by laws enacted by the two Houses of Congress, this fact did not necessarily subject their offices to congressional control, but, on the contrary, that "these instrumentalities were created for the benefit of the people, and to answer the general purposes of government under the Constitution and the laws; and that they are unencumbered by any lien in favor of either branch of Congress growing out of their construction, and unembarrassed by any obligation to the Senate as the price of their creation." While not conceding that the Senate had in any case the right to review Executive action in suspending officials, the President disclaimed any intention to withhold official papers and documents when requested; and as to such papers and documents, he expressed his willingness, because they were official, to continue, as he had theretofore done in all cases, to lay them before the Senate without inquiry as to the use to be made of them, and relying upon the Senate for their legitimate utilization. The proposition was expressly denied, however, that papers and documents inherently private or confidential, addressed to the President or a head of department, having reference to an act so entirely executive in its nature as the suspension of an official, and which was by the Constitution as well as by existing law placed within the discretion of the President, were changed in their nature and instantly became official when placed for convenience or for other reasons in the custody of a public department. The contention of the President was thus stated:

> There is no mysterious power of transmutation in departmental custody, nor is there magic in the undefined and sacred solemnity of departmental files. If the presence of these papers in the public office is a stumbling-block in the way of the performance of senatorial duty, it can be easily removed.

The Senate's purposes were characterized in the message as follows:

> The requests and demands which by the score have for nearly three months been presented to the different

departments of the Government, whatever may be their form, have but one complexion. They assume the right of the Senate to sit in judgment upon the exercise of my exclusive discretion and Executive function, for which I am solely responsible to the people from whom I have so lately received the sacred trust of office. My oath to support and defend the Constitution, my duty to the people who have chosen me to execute the powers of their great office and not relinquish them, and my duty to the chief magistracy which I must preserve unimpaired in all its dignity and vigor, compel me to refuse compliance with these demands.

This was immediately supplemented by the following concession of the independent and unlimited power of the Senate in the matter of confirmation:

To the end that the service may be improved, the Senate is invited to the fullest scrutiny of the persons submitted to them for public office, in recognition of the constitutional power of that body to advise and consent to their appointment. I shall continue, as I have thus far done, to furnish, at the request of the confirming body, all the information I possess touching the fitness of the nominees placed before them for their action, both when they are proposed to fill vacancies and to take the place of suspended officials. Upon a refusal to confirm, I shall not assume the right to ask the reasons for the action of the Senate nor question its determination. I cannot think that anything more is required to secure worthy incumbents in public office than a careful and independent discharge of our respective duties within their well-defined limits.

As it was hardly concealed that by no means the least important senatorial purpose in the pending controversy was to discredit the Civil Service reform pledges and professions of the Executive, this issue was thus distinctly invited at the close of the message:

Every pledge I have made by which I have placed a limitation upon my exercise of executive power has been faithfully redeemed. Of course the pretense is not put forth that no mistakes have been committed; but not a suspension has been made except it appeared to my satisfaction that the public welfare would be promoted thereby. Many applications for suspension have been denied, and an adherence to the rule laid down to govern my action as to such suspensions has caused much irritation and impatience on the part of those who have insisted upon more changes in the offices.

The pledges I have made were made to the people, and to them I am responsible for the manner in which they have been redeemed. I am not responsible to the Senate, and I am unwilling to submit my actions and official conduct to them for judgment.

There are no grounds for an allegation that the fear of being found false to my professions influences me in declining to submit to the demands of the Senate. I have not constantly refused to suspend officials and thus incurred the displeasure of political friends, and yet wilfully broken faith with the people, for the sake of being false to them.

Neither the discontent of party friends nor the allurements, constantly offered, of confirmation of appointees conditioned upon the avowal that suspensions have been made on party grounds alone, nor the threat proposed in the resolutions now before the Senate that no confirmation will be made unless the demands of that body be complied with, are sufficient to discourage or deter me from following in the way which I am convinced leads to better government for the people.

The temper and disposition of the Senate may be correctly judged, I think, from the remarks made upon the presentation of this message by the chairman of the Committee on the Judiciary and the acknowledged leader of the majority. On a formal motion that the message be printed and lie upon the table, he moved as an amendment that it be referred to the committee of which he was chairman, and said:

I merely wish to remark, in moving to refer this document to the Committee on the Judiciary, that it very vividly brought to my mind the communications of King Charles I to the Parliament, telling them what, in conducting their affairs, they ought to do and ought not to do; and I think I am safe in saying that it is the first time in the history of the republican United States that any President of the United States has undertaken to interfere with the deliberations of either House of Congress on questions pending before them, otherwise than by messages on the state of the Union which the Constitution commands him to make from time to time. This message is devoted simply to a question for the Senate itself, in regard to itself, that it has under consideration. That is its singularity. I think it will strike reflecting people in this country as somewhat extraordinary—if in this day of reform anything at all can be thought extraordinary.

King Charles I fared badly at the hands of the Parliament; but it was most reassuring to know that, after all said and done, the Senate of the United States was not a bloodthirsty body, and that the chairman of its Committee on the Judiciary was one of the most courteous and amiable of men—at least when outside of the Senate.

The debate upon the questions presented by the report and resolutions recommended by the majority of the committee, and by the minority report and the presidential message, occupied almost exclusively the sessions of the Senate for over two weeks. More than twenty-five Senators participated, and the discussion covered such a wide range of argument that all considerations relevant to the subject, and some not clearly related to it, seem to have been presented. At the close of the debate, the resolution condemning the Attorney-General for withholding the papers and documents which the Senate had demanded was passed by thirty-two votes in the affirmative and twenty-five in the negative; the next resolution, declaring it to be the duty of the Senate to refuse its advice and consent to proposed removals of officers when papers and documents in reference to their alleged misconduct were withheld, was adopted by a majority of only a single vote; and the proclamation contained in the third resolution, setting forth the obligations of the Government and its people to the veterans of the civil war, was unanimously approved, except for one dissenting voice.

The controversy thus closed arose from the professed anxiety of the majority in the Senate to guard the interests of an official who was suspended from office in July, 1885, and who was still claimed to be in a condition of suspension. In point of fact, however, that official's term of office expired by limitation on the 20th of December, 1885—before the demand for papers and documents relating to his conduct in office was made, before the resolutions and reports of the Committee on the Judiciary were presented, and before the commencement of the long discussion in defense of the right of a suspended incumbent. This situation escaped notice in Executive quarters, because the appointee to succeed the suspended officer having been actually installed and in the discharge of the duties of the position for more than six months, and his nomination having been sent to the Senate very soon after the beginning of its session, the situation or duration of the former incumbent's term was not kept in mind.

The expiration of his term was, however, distinctly alleged in the Senate on the second day of the discussion, and by the first speaker in opposition to the majority report. The question of suspension or removal was therefore eliminated from the case and the discussion as related to the person suspended continued as a sort of post-mortem proceeding. Shortly after the resolutions of the committee were passed, the same person who superseded the suspended and defunct officer was again nominated to succeed him by reason of the expiration of his term; and this nomination was confirmed.

At last, after stormy weather, Duskin, the suspended, and Burnett, his successor, were at rest. The earnest contention that beat about their names ceased, and no shout of triumph disturbed the supervening quiet.

V

I have thus attempted, after fourteen years of absolute calm, to recount the prominent details of the strife; and I hope that interest in the subject is still sufficient to justify me in a further brief reference to some features of the dispute and certain incidents that followed it, which may aid to a better appreciation of its true character and motive.

Of the elaborate speeches made in support of the resolutions and the committee's majority report, seven dealt more or less prominently with the President's Civil Service reform professions and his pledges against the removal of officials on purely partizan grounds. It seems to have been assumed that these pledges had been violated. At any rate, without any evidence worthy of the name, charges of such violation ranged all the way from genteel insinuation to savage accusation. Senators who would have stoutly refused to vote for the spoils system broadly intimated or openly declared that if suspensions had been made confessedly on partizan grounds they would have interposed no opposition. The majority seem to have especially admired and applauded the antics of one of their number, who, in intervals of lurid and indiscriminate vituperation, gleefully mingled ridicule for Civil Service reform with praise of the forbidding genius of partizan spoils. In view of these deliverances and as bearing upon their relevancy, as well as indicating their purpose, let me again suggest that the issue involved in the discussion as selected by the majority of the Committee on the Judiciary, and distinctly declared in their report, was whether, as a matter of right, or, as the report expresses it, as within "constitutional competence," either House of Congress should "have access to the official papers and documents in the various public offices of the United States, created by laws enacted by themselves." It will be readily seen that if the question was one of senatorial right, the President's Civil Service reform pledges had no honest or legitimate place in the discussion.

The debate and the adoption of the resolutions reported by the committee caused no surrender of the Executive position. Nevertheless, confirmations of those nominated in place of suspended officers soon began, and I cannot recall any further embarrassment or difficulty on that score. I ought to add, however, that in many cases, at least, these confirmations were accompanied by reports from the committee to which they had been referred, stating that the late incumbent had been suspended for "political reasons," or on account of "offensive partizanship," or for a like reason, differently expressed, and that nothing was alleged against them affecting their personal character. If the terms thus used by the committee in designating causes for suspension mean that the persons suspended were guilty of offensive partizanship or political offenses, as distinguished from personal offenses and moral or official delinquencies, I am satisfied with the statement. And here it occurs to me to suggest that if offenses and moral or official delinquencies, not partizan in their nature, had existed, they would have been subjects for official inspection and report, and such reports, being official documents, would have been submitted to the committee or to the Senate, according to custom, and would have told their own story and excluded committee comment.

It is worth recalling, when referring to committee reports on nomination, that they belong to the executive business of the Senate, and are, therefore, among the secrets of that body. Those I have mentioned, nevertheless, were by special order made public, and published in the proceedings of the Senate in open session. This extraordinary, if not unprecedented, action, following long after the conclusion of the dispute, easily interprets its own intent, and removes all covering from a design to accomplish partizan advantage. The declaration of the resolutions that it was the duty of the Senate "to refuse its advice and consent to the proposed removal of officers" when the papers and documents relating to their supposed misconduct were withheld, was abandoned, and the irrevocable removal of such officers by confirmation of their successors was entered upon, with or without the much-desired papers and documents, and was supplemented by the publication of committee reports, from which the secrecy of the executive session had been removed, to the end that, pursuant to a fixed determination, an unfavorable senatorial interpretation might be publicly given to the President's action in making suspensions.

I desire to call attention to one other incident connected with the occurrences already narrated. On the 14th of December, 1885,—prior to the first request or demand upon any executive department relating to suspensions, and of course before any controversy upon the subject arose,—a bill was introduced in the Senate by one of the most distinguished and able members of the majority in that body, and also a member of its Committee on the Judiciary, for the total and complete repeal of the law of 1869, which, it will be remembered, furnished the basis for the contention we have considered. This repealing bill was referred to the Senate Committee on the Judiciary, where it slumbered until the 21st of June, 1886,—nearly three months after the close of the contention,—when it was returned to the Senate with a favorable report, the chairman of the committee alone dissenting. When the bill was presented for discussion, the Senator who introduced it explained its object as follows:

> This bill repeals what is left of what is called the Tenure of Office act, passed under the administration of Andrew Johnson, and as a part of the contest with that President. It leaves the law as it was from the beginning of the Government until that time, and it repeals the provision which authorizes the suspension of civil officers and requires the submission of that suspension to the Senate.

On a later day, in discussing the bill, he said, after referring to the early date of its introduction:

> It did not seem to me to be quite becoming to ask the Senate to deal with this general question while the question which arose between the President and the Senate as to the interpretation and administration of the existing law was pending. I thought as a party man that I had hardly the right to interfere with the matter which was under the special charge of my honorable friend from Vermont, by challenging a debate upon the general subject from a different point of view. This question has subsided and is past, and it seems to me now proper to ask the Senate to vote upon the question whether it will return to the ancient policy of the Government, to the rule of public conduct which existed from 1789 until 1867, and which has practically existed, notwithstanding the condition of the statute-book, since the accession to power of General Grant on the 4th of March, 1869.

The personnel of the committee which reported favorably upon this repealing bill had not been changed since all the members of it politically affiliating with the majority in the Senate joined in recommending the accusatory report and resolutions, which, when adopted, after sharp and irritating discussion, caused the question between the President and the Senate, in the language of the introducer of the repealing bill, to "subside."

This repealing act passed the Senate on the 17th of December, 1886, by thirty affirmative votes against twenty-two in the negative. A short time afterward it passed in the House of Representatives by a majority of one hundred and five.

Thus was an unpleasant controversy happily followed by an expurgation of the last pretense of statutory sanction to an encroachment upon constitutional Executive prerogatives, and thus was a time-honored interpretation of the Constitution restored to us. The President, freed from the Senate's claim of tutelage, became again the independent agent of the people, representing a coördinate branch of their Government, charged with responsibilities which, under his oath, he ought not to avoid or divide with others, and invested with powers, not to be surrendered, but to be used, under the guidance of patriotic intention and an unclouded conscience.

THE GOVERNMENT IN THE CHICAGO STRIKE OF 1894

I

The President inaugurated on the fourth day of March, 1893, and those associated with him as Cabinet officials, encountered, during their term of executive duty, unusual and especially perplexing difficulties. The members of that administration who still survive, in recalling the events of this laborious service, cannot fail to fix upon the years 1894 and 1895 as the most troublous and anxious of their incumbency. During those years unhappy currency complications compelled executive resort to heroic treatment for the preservation of our nation's financial integrity, and forced upon the administration a constant, unrelenting struggle for sound money; a long and persistent executive effort to accomplish beneficent and satisfactory tariff reform so nearly miscarried as to bring depression and disappointment to the verge of discouragement; and it was at the close of the year 1895 that executive insistence upon the Monroe Doctrine culminated in a situation that gave birth to solemn thoughts of war. Without attempting to complete the list of troubles and embarrassments that beset the administration during these luckless years, I have reserved for separate and more detailed treatment one of its incidents not yet mentioned, which immensely increased executive anxiety and foreboded the most calamitous and far-reaching consequences.

In the last days of June, 1894, a very determined and ugly labor disturbance broke out in the city of Chicago. Almost in a night it grew to full proportions of malevolence and danger. Rioting and violence were its early accompaniments; and it spread so swiftly that within a few days it had reached nearly the entire Western and Southwestern sections of our country. Railroad transportation was especially involved in its attacks. The carriage of United States mails was interrupted, interstate commerce was obstructed, and railroad property was riotously destroyed.

This disturbance is often called "The Chicago Strike." It is true that its beginning was in that city; and the headquarters of those who inaugurated it and directed its operations were located there; but the name thus given to it is an entire misnomer so far as it applies to the scope and reach of the trouble. Railroad operations were more or less affected in twenty-seven States and Territories; and in all these the interposition of the general Government was to a greater or less extent invoked.

This wide-spread trouble had its inception in a strike by the employees of the Pullman Palace Car Company, a corporation located and doing business at the town of Pullman, which is within the limits of the city of Chicago. This company was a manufacturing corporation—or at least it was not a railroad corporation. Its main object was the operation and running of sleeping- and parlor-cars upon railroads under written contracts; but its charter contemplated the manufacture of cars as well; and soon after its incorporation it began the manufacture of its own cars and, subsequently, the manufacture of cars for the general market.

The strike on the part of the employees of this company began on the eleventh day of May, 1894, and was provoked by a reduction of wages.

The American Railway Union was organized in the summer of 1893. It was professedly an association of all the different classes of railway employees. In its scope and intent it was the most compact and effective organization of the kind ever attempted. Its purpose was a thorough unification of defensive and offensive effort among railway employees under one central direction, and the creation of a combination embracing all such employees, which should make the grievances of any section of its membership a common cause. Those prominent in this project estimated that various other organizations of railroad employees then existing had a membership of 102,000 in the United States and neighboring countries; and they claimed that these brotherhoods, because of divided councils and for other reasons, were ineffective, and that nearly 1,000,000 railroad employees still remained unorganized.

The wonderful growth of this new combination is made apparent by the fact that between the month of August, 1893, and the time it became involved in the Pullman strike, in June, 1894, it had enrolled nearly 150,000 members.

The employees of the Pullman Palace Car Company could not on any reasonable and consistent theory be regarded as eligible to membership in an organization devoted to the interests of railway employees; and yet, during the months of March, April, and May, 1894, it appears that nearly 4000 of these employees were enrolled in the American Railway Union.

This, to say the least of it, was an exceedingly unfortunate proceeding, since it created a situation which implicated in a comparatively insignificant quarrel between the managers of an industrial establishment and their workmen the large army of the Railway Union. It was the membership of these workmen in the Railway Union, and the union's consequent assumption of their quarrel, that gave it the proportions of a tremendous disturbance, paralyzing the most important business interests, obstructing the functions of the Government, and disturbing social peace and order....

No injury to the property of the Pullman Palace Car Company was done or attempted while the strike was confined to its employees; and during that time very little disorder of any kind occurred.

It so happened, however, that in June, 1894, after the strike at Pullman had continued for about one month, a regular stated convention of the American Railway Union was held in the city of Chicago, which was attended by delegates from local branches of the organization in different States, as well as by representatives of its members among the employees of the Pullman Palace Car Company. At this convention the trouble at Pullman was considered, and after earnest efforts on the part of the Railway Union to bring about a settlement, a resolution was, on the twenty-second day of June, passed by the convention, declaring that unless the Pullman Palace Car Company should adjust the grievances of its employees before noon of the twenty-sixth day of June, the members of the American Railway Union would, after that date, refuse to handle Pullman cars and equipment.

The twenty-sixth day of June arrived without any change in the attitude of the parties to the Pullman controversy; and thereupon the order made by the American Railway Union forbidding the handling of Pullman cars, became operative throughout its entire membership.

At this time the Pullman Palace Car Company was furnishing drawing-room and sleeping-car accommodations to the traveling public under contracts with numerous railway companies, and was covering by this service about one hundred and twenty-five thousand miles of railway, or approximately three fourths of all the railroad mileage of the country. The same railroad companies which had contracted to use these Pullman cars upon their lines had contracts with the United States Government for the carriage of mails, and were, of course, also largely engaged in interstate commerce. It need hardly be said that, of necessity, the trains on which the mails were carried and which served the purpose of interstate commerce were, very generally, those to which the Pullman cars were also attached.

The president of the Railway Union was one Eugene V. Debs. In a sworn statement afterward made he gave the following description of the results of the interference of the union in the Pullman dispute:

> The employees, obedient to the order of the convention, at once, on the 26th, refused to haul Pullman cars. The switchmen, in the first place, refused to attach a Pullman car to a train, and that is where the trouble began; and then, when a switchman would be discharged for that, they would all simultaneously quit, as they had agreed to do. One department after another was involved until the

Illinois Central was practically paralyzed, and the Rock Island and other roads in their turn. Up to the first day of July, or after the strike had been in progress five days, the railway managers, as we believe, were completely defeated. Their immediate resources were exhausted, their properties were paralyzed, and they were unable to operate their trains. Our men were intact at every point, firm, quiet, and yet determined, and no sign of violence or disorder anywhere. That was the condition on the thirtieth day of June and the first day of July.

The officers of the Railway Union from their headquarters in the city of Chicago gave directions for the maintenance and management of the strike, which were quickly transmitted to distant railroad points and were there promptly executed. As early as the 28th of June, two days after the beginning of the strike ordered by the Railway Union at Chicago, information was received at Washington from the Post-Office Department that on the Southern Pacific System, between Portland and San Francisco, Ogden and San Francisco, and Los Angeles and San Francisco, the mails were completely obstructed, and that the strikers refused to permit trains to which Pullman cars were attached to run over the lines mentioned. Thereupon Attorney-General Olney immediately sent the following telegraphic despatch to the United States district attorneys in the State of California:

WASHINGTON, D. C., June 28, 1894.

See that the passage of regular trains, carrying United States mails in the usual and ordinary way, as contemplated by the act of Congress and directed by the Postmaster-General, is not obstructed. Procure warrants or any other available process from United States courts against any and all persons engaged in such obstructions, and direct the marshal to execute the same by such number of deputies or such posse as may be necessary.

On the same day, and during a number of days immediately following, complaints of a similar character, sometimes accompanied by charges of forcible seizure of trains and other violent disorders, poured in upon the Attorney-General from all parts of the West and Southwest. These complaints came from post-office officials, from United States marshals and district attorneys, from railroad managers, and from other officials and private citizens. In all cases of substantial representation of interference with the carriage of mails, a despatch identical with that already quoted was sent by the Attorney-General to the United States district attorneys in the disturbed localities; and this was supplemented, whenever necessary, by such other prompt action as the different emergencies required.

I shall not enter upon an enumeration of all the disorders and violence, the defiance of law and authority, and the obstructions of national functions and duties, which occurred in many localities as a consequence of this labor contention, thus tremendously reinforced and completely under way. It is my especial purpose to review the action taken by the Government for the maintenance of its own authority and the protection of the interests intrusted to its keeping, so far as they were endangered by this disturbance; and I do not intend to specifically deal with the incidents of the strike except in so far as a reference to them may be necessary to show conditions which not only justified but actually obliged the Government to resort to stern and unusual measures in the assertion of its prerogatives.

Inasmuch, therefore, as the city of Chicago was the birthplace of the disturbance and the home of its activities, and because it was the field of its most pronounced and malign manifestations, as well as the place of its final extinction, I shall meet the needs of my subject if I supplement what has been already said by a recital of events occurring at this central point. In doing this, I shall liberally embody documents, orders, instructions, and reports which I hope will not prove tiresome, since they supply the facts I desire to present, at first hand and more impressively than they could be presented by any words of mine.

Owing to the enforced relationship of Chicago to the strike which started within its borders, and because of its importance as a center of railway traffic, Government officials at Washington were not surprised by the early and persistent complaints of mail and interstate commerce obstructions which reached them from that city. It was from the first anticipated that this would be the seat of the most serious complications, and the place where the strong arm of the law would be most needed. In these circumstances it would have been a criminal neglect of duty if those charged with the protection of governmental agencies and the enforcement of orderly obedience and submission to Federal authority, had been remiss in preparations for any emergency in that quarter.

On the thirtieth day of June the district attorney at Chicago reported by telegraph that mail trains in the suburbs of Chicago were, on the previous night, stopped by strikers, that an engine had been cut off and disabled, and that conditions were growing more and more likely to culminate in the stoppage of all trains; and he recommended that the marshal be authorized to employ a force of special deputies who should be placed on trains to protect mails and detect the parties guilty of such interference. In reply to this despatch Attorney-General Olney on the same day authorized the marshal to employ additional deputies as suggested, and designated Edwin Walker, an able and prominent attorney in Chicago, as special counsel for the Government, to assist the district attorney in any legal proceedings that might be instituted. He also notified the district attorney of the steps thus taken, and enjoined upon him that "action ought to be prompt and vigorous," and also directed him to confer with the special counsel who had been employed. In a letter of the same date addressed to this special counsel, the Attorney-General, in making suggestions concerning legal proceedings, wrote: "It has seemed to me that if the rights of the United States were vigorously asserted in Chicago, the origin and center of the demonstration, the result would be to make it a failure everywhere else, and to prevent its spread over the entire country"; and in that connection he indicated that it might be advisable, instead of relying entirely upon warrants issued under criminal statutes against persons actually guilty of the offense of obstructing United States mails, to apply to the courts for injunctions which would restrain and prevent any attempt to commit such offense. This suggestion contemplated the inauguration of legal proceedings in a regular and usual way to restrain those prominently concerned in the interference with the mails and the obstruction of interstate commerce, basing such proceedings on the proposition that, under the Constitution and laws, these subjects were in the exclusive care of the Government of the United States, and that for their protection the Federal courts were competent under general principles of law to intervene by injunction; and on the further ground that under an act of Congress, passed July 2, 1890, conspiracies in restraint of trade or commerce among the several States were declared to be illegal, and the circuit courts of the United States were therein expressly given jurisdiction to prevent and restrain such conspiracies.

On the first day of July the district attorney reported to the Attorney-General that he was preparing a bill of complaint to be presented to the court the next day, on an application for an injunction. He further reported that very little mail and no freight was moving, that the marshal was using all his force to prevent riots and the obstruction of tracks, and that this force was clearly inadequate. On the same day the marshal reported that the situation was desperate, that he had sworn in over four hundred deputies, that many more would be required to protect mail trains, and that he expected great trouble the next day. He further expressed the opinion that one hundred riot guns were needed.

Upon the receipt of these reports, and anticipating an attempt to serve injunctions on the following day, the Attorney-General immediately sent a despatch to the district attorney directing him to report at once if the process of the court should be resisted by such force as the marshal could not overcome, and suggesting that the United States judge should join in such report. He at the same time sent a despatch to the special counsel requesting him to report his view of the situation as early as the forenoon of the next day.

In explanation of these two despatches it should here be said that the desperate character of this disturbance was not in the least underestimated by executive officials at Washington; and it must be borne in mind that while menacing conditions were moving swiftly and accumulating at Chicago, like conditions, inspired and supported from that central point, existed in many other places within the area of the strike's contagion.

Of course it was hoped by those charged with the responsibility of dealing with the situation, that a direct assertion of authority by the marshal and a resort to the restraining power of the courts would prove sufficient for the emergency. Notwithstanding, however, an anxious desire to avoid measures more radical, the fact had not been overlooked that a contingency might occur which would compel a resort to military force. The key to these despatches of the Attorney-General is found in the determination of the Federal authorities to overcome by any lawful and constitutional means all resistance to governmental functions as related to the transportation of mails, the operation of interstate commerce, and the preservation of the property of the United States.

The Constitution requires that the United States shall protect each of the States against invasion, "and on application of the legislature, or of the executive (when the legislature cannot be convened), against domestic violence." There was plenty of domestic violence in the city of Chicago and in the State of Illinois during the early days of July, 1894; but no application was made to the Federal Government for assistance. It was probably a very fortunate circumstance that the presence of United States soldiers in Chicago at that time did not depend upon the request or desire of Governor Altgeld.

Section 5298 of the Revised Statutes of the United States provides: "Whenever, by reason of unlawful obstructions, combinations or assemblages of persons, or rebellion against the authority of the United States, it shall become impracticable in the judgment of the President to enforce, by the ordinary course of judicial proceedings, the laws of the United States within any State or Territory, it shall be lawful for the President to call forth the militia of any or all of the States, and to employ such parts of the land or naval forces of the United States as he may deem necessary to enforce the faithful execution of the laws of the United States, or to suppress such rebellion, in whatever State or Territory thereof the laws of the United States may be forcibly opposed, or the execution thereof be forcibly obstructed"; and Section 5299 provides: "Whenever any insurrection, domestic violence, unlawful combinations or conspiracies in any State ... opposes or obstructs the laws of the United States, or the due execution thereof, or impedes or obstructs the due course of justice under the same, it shall be lawful for the President, and it shall be his duty, to take such measures, by the employment of the militia, or the land and naval forces of the United States, or of either, or by other means as he may deem necessary, for the suppression of such insurrection, domestic violence or combinations."

<hr>

II

It was the intention of the Attorney-General to suggest in these despatches that immediate and authoritative information should be given to the Washington authorities if a time should arrive when, under the sanction of general executive authority, or the constitutional and statutory provisions above quoted, a military force would be necessary at the scene of disturbance.

On the 2d of July, the day after these despatches were sent, information was received from the district attorney and special counsel that a sweeping injunction had been granted against Eugene V. Debs, president of the American Railway Union, and other officials of that organization, together with parties whose names were unknown, and that the writs would be served that afternoon. The special counsel also expressed the opinion that it would require Government troops to enforce the orders of the court and protect the transportation of mails.

Major-General Schofield was then in command of the army; and, after a consultation with him, in which the Attorney-General and the Secretary of War took part, I directed the issuance of the following order by telegraph to General Nelson A. Miles, in command of the Military Department of Missouri, with headquarters at Chicago:

HEADQUARTERS OF THE ARMY.
WASHINGTON, July 2, 1894.

To the Commanding-General,
Department of Missouri,
Chicago, Ill.

You will please make all necessary arrangements confidentially for the transportation of the entire garrison at Fort Sheridan—infantry, cavalry, and artillery—to the lake front in the city of Chicago. To avoid possible interruption of the movement by rail and by marching through a part of the city, it may be advisable to bring them by steam-boat. Please consider this matter and have the arrangements perfected without delay. You may expect orders at any time for the movement. Acknowledge receipt and report in what manner movement is to be made.

> J. M. SCHOFIELD,
> *Major-General Commanding.*

It should by no means be inferred from this despatch that it had been definitely determined that the use of a military force was inevitable. It was still hoped that the effect of the injunction would be such that this alternative might be avoided. A painful emergency is created when public duty forces the necessity of placing trained soldiers face to face with riotous opposition to the general Government, and an acute and determined defiance to law and order. This course, once entered upon, admits of no backward step; and an appreciation of the consequences that may ensue cannot fail to oppress those responsible for its adoption with sadly disturbing reflections. Nevertheless, it was perfectly plain that, whatever the outcome might be, the situation positively demanded such precaution and preparation as would insure readiness and promptness in case the presence of a military force should finally be found necessary.

On the morning of the next day, July 3, the Attorney-General received a letter from Mr. Walker, the special counsel, in which, after referring to the issuance of the injunctions and setting forth that the marshal was engaged in serving them, he wrote:

> I do not believe that the marshal and his deputies can protect the railroad companies in moving their trains, either freight or passenger, including, of course, the trains carrying United States mails. Possibly, however, the service of the writ of injunction will have a restraining influence upon Debs and other officers of the association. If it does not, from present appearances, I think it is the opinion of all that the orders of the court cannot be enforced except by the aid of the regular army.

Thereupon the Attorney-General immediately sent this despatch to the district attorney:

> I trust use of United States troops will not be necessary. If it becomes necessary, they will be used promptly and decisively upon the justifying facts being certified to me.

In such case, if practicable, let Walker and the marshal and United States judge join in statement as to the exigency.

A few hours afterward the following urgent and decisive despatch from the marshal, endorsed by a judge of the United States court and the district attorney and special counsel, was received by the Attorney-General.

CHICAGO, ILL., July 3, 1894.

Hon. RICHARD OLNEY, *Attorney-General,*
Washington, D. C.:

When the injunction was granted yesterday, a mob of from two to three thousand held possession of a point in the city near the crossing of the Rock Island by other roads, where they had already ditched a mail-train, and prevented the passing of any trains, whether mail or otherwise. I read the injunction writ to this mob and commanded them to disperse. The reading of the writ met with no response except jeers and hoots. Shortly after, the mob threw a number of baggage-cars across the track, since when no mail-train has been able to move. I am unable to disperse the mob, clear the tracks, or arrest the men who were engaged in the acts named, and believe that no force less than the regular troops of the United States can procure the passage of the mail-trains, or enforce the orders of the courts. I believe people engaged in trades are quitting employment to-day, and in my opinion will be joining the mob to-night and especially to-morrow; and it is my judgment that the troops should be here at the earliest moment. An emergency has arisen for their presence in this city.

J. W. ARNOLD,
United States Marshal.

We have read the foregoing, and from that information, and other information that has come to us, believe that an emergency exists for the immediate presence of United States troops.

P. S. GROSSCUP, *Judge.*

EDWIN WALKER,

Attys.

THOMAS E. MILCHIST,

In the afternoon of the same day the following order was telegraphed from army headquarters in the city of Washington:

WAR DEPARTMENT,
HEADQUARTERS OF THE ARMY.
WASHINGTON, D. C., July 3, 1894,
4 o'clock P.M.

TO   MARTIN,   *Adjutant-General,*
Headquarters Department of Missouri,

Chicago, Ill.

It having become impracticable in the judgment of the President to enforce by the ordinary course of judicial proceedings the laws of the United States, you will direct Colonel Crofton to move his entire command at once to the city of Chicago (leaving the necessary guard at Fort Sheridan), there to execute the orders and processes of the United States court, to prevent the obstruction of the United States mails, and generally to enforce the faithful execution of the laws of the United States. He will confer with the United States marshal, the United States district attorney, and Edwin Walker, special counsel. Acknowledge receipt and report action promptly. By order of the President.

J. M. SCHOFIELD, *Major-General.*

Immediately after this order was issued, the following despatch was sent to the district attorney by the Attorney-General:

Colonel Crofton's command ordered to Chicago by the President. As to disposition and movement of troops, yourself, Walker, and the marshal should confer with Colonel Crofton and with Colonel Martin, adjutant-general at Chicago. While action should be prompt and decisive, it should of course be kept within the limits provided by the Constitution and laws. Rely upon yourself and Walker to see that this is done.

Colonel Martin, adjutant-general at Chicago, reported, the same night at half-past nine o'clock, that the order for the movement of troops was, immediately on its receipt by him, transmitted to Fort Sheridan, and that Colonel Crofton's command started for Chicago at nine o'clock.

During the forenoon of the next day, July 4, Colonel Martin advised the War Department that Colonel Crofton reported his command in the city of Chicago at 10:15 that morning. After referring to the manner in which the troops had been distributed, this officer added: "People seem to feel easier since arrival of troops."

General Miles, commanding the department, arrived in Chicago the same morning, and at once assumed direction of military movements. In the afternoon of that day he sent a report to the War Department at Washington, giving an account of the disposition of troops, recounting an unfavorable condition of affairs, and recommending an increase of the garrison at Fort Sheridan sufficient to meet any emergency.

In response to this despatch General Miles was immediately authorized to order six companies of infantry from Fort Leavenworth, in Kansas, and two companies from Fort Brady, in Michigan, to Fort Sheridan.

On the fifth day of July he reported that a mob of over two thousand had gathered that morning at the stock-yards, crowded among the troops, obstructed the movement of trains, knocked down a railroad official, and overturned about twenty freight-cars, which obstructed all freight and passenger traffic in the vicinity of the stock-yards, and that the mob had also derailed a passenger-train on the Pittsburg, Fort Wayne and Chicago Railroad, and burned switches. To this recital of violent demonstrations he added the following statement:

> The injunction of the United States court is openly defied, and unless the mobs are dispersed by the action of the police or they are fired upon by United States troops, more serious trouble may be expected, as the mob is increasing and becoming more defiant.

In view of the situation as reported by General Miles, a despatch was sent to him by General Schofield directing him to concentrate his troops in order that they might act more effectively in the execution of orders theretofore given, and in the protection of United States property. This despatch concluded as follows:

> The mere preservation of peace and good order in the city is, of course, the province of the city and state authorities.

The situation on the sixth day of July was thus described in a despatch sent in the afternoon of that day by General Miles to the Secretary of War:

In answer to your telegram, I report the following: Mayor Hopkins last night issued a proclamation prohibiting riotous assemblies and directing the police to stop people from molesting railway communication. Governor Altgeld has ordered General Wheeler's brigade on duty in Chicago to support the Mayor's authority. So far, there have been no large mobs like the one of yesterday, which moved from 51st Street to 18th Street before it dispersed. The lawlessness has been along the line of the railways, destroying and burning more than one hundred cars and railway buildings, and obstructing transportation in various ways, even to the extent of cutting telegraph lines. United States troops have dispersed mobs at 51st Street, Kensington, and a company of infantry is moving along the Rock Island to support a body of United States marshals in making arrests for violating the injunction of the United States court. Of the twenty-three roads centering in Chicago, only six are unobstructed in freight, passenger, and mail transportation. Thirteen are at present entirely obstructed, and ten are running only mail- and passenger-trains. Large numbers of trains moving in and out of the city have been stoned and fired upon by mobs, and one engineer killed. There was a secret meeting to-day of Debs and the representatives of labor unions considering the advisability of a general strike of all labor unions. About one hundred men were present at that meeting. The result is not yet known. United States troops are at the stock-yards, Kensington, Blue Island, crossing of 51st Street, and have been moving along some of the lines: the balance, eight companies of infantry, battery of artillery, and one troop of cavalry, are camped on Lake Front Park, ready for any emergency and to protect Government buildings and property. It is learned from the Fire Department, City Hall, that a party of strikers has been going through the vicinity from 14th to 41st streets and Stewart Avenue freight-yards, throwing gasoline on freight-cars all through that section. Captain Ford, of the Fire Department, was badly stoned this morning. Troops have just dispersed a mob of incendiaries on Fort Wayne tracks, near 51st Street, and fires that were started have been suppressed. Mob just captured mail-train at 47th Street, and troops sent to disperse them.

On the eighth day of July, in view of the apparently near approach of a crisis which the Government had attempted to avoid, the following Executive Proclamation was issued and at once extensively published in the city of Chicago:

> Whereas, by reason of unlawful obstruction, combinations and assemblages of persons, it has become impracticable, in the judgment of the President, to enforce, by the ordinary course of judicial proceedings, the laws of the United States within the State of Illinois, and especially in the city of Chicago within said State; and

> Whereas, for the purpose of enforcing the faithful execution of the laws of the United States and protecting its property and removing obstructions to the United States mails in the State and city aforesaid, the President has employed a part of the military forces of the United States:—

> Now, therefore, I, Grover Cleveland, President of the United States, do hereby admonish all good citizens, and all persons who may be or may come within the City and State aforesaid, against aiding, countenancing, encouraging, or taking any part in such unlawful obstructions, combinations, and assemblages; and I hereby warn all persons engaged in or in any way connected with such unlawful obstructions, combinations, and assemblages to disperse and retire peaceably to their respective abodes on or before twelve o'clock noon of the 9th day of July instant.

> Those who disregard this warning and persist in taking part with a riotous mob in forcibly resisting and obstructing the execution of the laws of the United States, or interfering with the functions of the Government, or destroying or attempting to destroy the property belonging to the United States or under its protection, cannot be regarded otherwise than as public enemies.

> Troops employed against such a riotous mob will act with all the moderation and forbearance consistent with the accomplishment of the desired end; but the stern necessities that confront them will not with certainty permit discrimination between guilty participants and those who are mingling with them from curiosity and without criminal intent. The only safe course, therefore,

for those not actually participating, is to abide at their homes, or at least not to be found in the neighborhood of riotous assemblages.

While there will be no vacillation in the decisive treatment of the guilty, this warning is especially intended to protect and save the innocent.

On the 10th of July, Eugene V. Debs, the president of the American Railway Union, together with its vice-president, general secretary, and one other who was an active director, were arrested upon indictments found against them for complicity in the obstruction of mails and interstate commerce. Three days afterward our special counsel expressed the opinion that the strike was practically broken. This must not be taken to mean, however, that peace and quiet had been completely restored or that the transportation of mails and the activities of interstate commerce were entirely free from interruption. It was only the expression of a well-sustained and deliberate expectation that the combination of measures already inaugurated, and others contemplated in the near future, would speedily bring about a termination of the difficulty.

On the seventeenth day of July an information was filed in the United States Circuit Court at Chicago against Debs and the three other officials of the Railway Union who had been arrested on indictment a few days before, but were then at large on bail. This information alleged that these parties had been guilty of open, continued, and defiant disobedience of the injunction which was served on them July 3, forbidding them to do certain specified acts tending to incite and aid the obstruction of the carriage of mails and the operation of interstate commerce. On the footing of this information these parties were brought before the court to show cause why they should not be punished for contempt in disobeying the injunction. Instead of giving bail for their freedom pending the investigation of this charge against them, as they were invited to do, they preferred to be committed to custody—perhaps intending by such an act of martyrdom either to revive a waning cause, or to gain a plausible and justifying excuse for the collapse of their already foredoomed movement. Debs himself, in speaking of this event afterward, said: "As soon as the employees found that we were arrested and taken from the scene of action they became demoralized, and that ended the strike."

That the strike ended about the time of this second arrest is undoubtedly true; for, during the few days immediately preceding and following the seventeenth day of July, reports came from nearly all the localities to which the strike had spread, indicating its defeat and the accomplishment of all the purposes of the Government's interference. The successful assertion of national authority was conclusively indicated when on the twentieth day of July the last of the soldiers of the United States who had been ordered for duty at the very center of opposition and disturbance, were withdrawn from Chicago and returned to the military posts to which they were attached.

I hope I have been successful thus far in my effort satisfactorily to exhibit the extensive reach and perilous tendency of the convulsion under consideration, the careful promptness which characterized the interference of the Government, the constant desire of the national administration to avoid extreme measures, the scrupulous limitation of its interference to purposes which were clearly within its constitutional competency and duty, and the gratifying and important results of its conservative but stern activity.

I must not fail to mention here as part of the history of this perplexing affair, a contribution made by the governor of Illinois to its annoyances. This official not only refused to regard the riotous disturbances within the borders of his State as a sufficient cause for an application to the Federal Government for its protection "against domestic violence" under the mandate of the Constitution, but he actually protested against the presence of Federal troops sent into the State upon the general Government's own initiative and for the purpose of defending itself in the exercise of its well-defined legitimate functions.

On the fifth day of July, twenty-four hours after our soldiers had been brought to the city of Chicago, pursuant to the order of July 3d, I received a long despatch from Governor Altgeld, beginning as follows:

> I am advised that you have ordered Federal troops to go into service in the State of Illinois. Surely the facts have not been correctly presented to you in this case or you would not have taken the step; for it is entirely unnecessary and, as it seems to me, unjustifiable. Waiving all question of courtesy, I will say that the State of Illinois is not only able to take care of itself, but it stands ready to-day to furnish the Federal Government any assistance it may need elsewhere.

This opening sentence was followed by a lengthy statement which so far missed actual conditions as to appear irrelevant and, in some parts, absolutely frivolous.

This remarkable despatch closed with the following words:

> As Governor of the State of Illinois, I protest against this and ask the immediate withdrawal of Federal troops from

active duty in this State. Should the situation at any time get so serious that we cannot control it with the State forces, we will promptly and freely ask for Federal assistance; but until such time I protest with all due deference against this uncalled-for reflection upon our people, and again ask for the immediate withdrawal of these troops.

Immediately upon the receipt of this communication, I sent to Governor Altgeld the following reply:

Federal troops were sent to Chicago in strict accordance with the Constitution and the laws of the United States, upon the demand of the Post-Office Department that obstructions of the mails should be removed, and upon the representation of the judicial officers of the United States that process of the Federal courts could not be executed through the ordinary means, and upon abundant proof that conspiracies existed against commerce between the States. To meet these conditions, which are clearly within the province of Federal authority, the presence of Federal troops in the city of Chicago was deemed not only proper but necessary; and there has been no intention of thereby interfering with the plain duty of the local authorities to preserve the peace of the city.

III

In response to this the governor, evidently unwilling to allow the matter at issue between us to rest without a renewal of argument and protest, at once addressed to me another long telegraphic communication, evidently intended to be more severely accusatory and insistent than its predecessor. Its general tenor may be inferred from the opening words:

Your answer to my protest involves some startling conclusions, and ignores and evades the question at issue—that is, that the principle of local self-government is just as fundamental in our institutions as is that of Federal supremacy. You calmly assume that the Executive has the legal right to order Federal troops into any community of the United States in the first instance, whenever there is the slightest disturbance, and that he can do this without any regard to the question as to whether the community is able to and ready to enforce the law itself.

After a rather dreary discussion of the importance of preserving the rights of the States and a presentation of the dangers to constitutional government that lurked in the course that had been pursued by the general Government, this communication closed as follows:

> Inasmuch as the Federal troops can do nothing but what the State troops can do there, and believing that the State is amply able to take care of the situation and to enforce the law, and believing that the ordering out of the Federal troops was unwarranted, I again ask their withdrawal.

I confess that my patience was somewhat strained when I quickly sent the following despatch in reply to this communication:

EXECUTIVE MANSION.
WASHINGTON, D. C., July 6, 1894.

> While I am still persuaded that I have neither transcended my authority nor duty in the emergency that confronts us, it seems to me that in this hour of danger and public distress, discussion may well give way to active efforts on the part of all in authority to restore obedience to law and to protect life and property.

GROVER CLEVELAND.

Hon. John P. Altgeld,
Governor of Illinois.

This closed a discussion which in its net results demonstrated how far one's disposition and inclination will lead him astray in the field of argument.

I shall conclude the treatment of my subject by a brief reference to the legal proceedings which grew out of this disturbance, and finally led to an adjudication by the highest court in our land, establishing in an absolutely authoritative manner and for all time the power of the national Government to protect itself in the exercise of its functions.

It will be recalled that in the course of our narrative we left Mr. Debs, the president of the Railway Union, and his three associates in custody of the law, on the seventeenth day of July, awaiting an investigation of the charge of contempt of court made against them, based upon their disobedience of the writs of injunction forbidding them to do certain things in aid or encouragement of interference with mail transportation or interstate commerce.

This investigation was so long delayed that the decision of the Circuit Court before which the proceedings were pending was not rendered until the fourteenth day of December, 1894. On that date the court delivered an able and carefully considered decision finding Debs and his associates guilty of contempt of court, basing its decision upon the provisions of the law of Congress, passed in 1890, entitled: "An act to protect trade and commerce against unlawful restraint and monopolies"; sometimes called the Sherman Anti-Trust Law. Thereupon the parties were sentenced on said conviction to confinement in the county jail for terms varying from three to six months.

Afterward, and on the 14th day of January, 1895, the prisoners applied to the Supreme Court of the United States for a writ of habeas corpus to relieve them from imprisonment, on the ground that the facts found against them by the Circuit Court did not constitute disobedience of the writs of injunction and that their commitment in the manner and for the reasons alleged was without justification and not within the constitutional power and jurisdiction of that tribunal.

On this application, the case was elaborately argued before the Supreme Court in March, 1895; and on the twenty-seventh day of May, 1895, the court rendered its decision, upholding on the broadest grounds the proceedings of the Circuit Court and confirming its adjudication and the commitment to jail of the petitioners thereupon.

Justice Brewer, in delivering the unanimous opinion of the Supreme Court, stated the case as follows:

> The United States, finding that the interstate transportation of persons and property, as well as the carriage of mails, is forcibly obstructed, and that a combination and conspiracy exists to subject the control of such transportation to the will of the conspirators, applied to one of their courts sitting as a court of equity, for an injunction to restrain such obstructions and prevent carrying into effect such conspiracy. Two questions of importance are presented: First, are the relations of the general Government to interstate commerce and the transportation of the mails such as to authorize a direct interference to prevent a forcible obstruction thereof? Second, if authority exists,—as authority in governmental affairs implies both power and duty,—has a court of equity jurisdiction to issue an injunction in aid of the performance of such duty?

Both of these questions were answered by the court in the affirmative; and in the opinion read by the learned justice, the inherent power of the Government to execute the powers and functions belonging to it by means of physical force through its official agents, and on every foot of American soil, was amply vindicated by a process of reasoning simple, logical, unhampered by fanciful distinctions, and absolutely conclusive; and the Government's peaceful resort to the court, the injunction issued in its aid, and all the proceedings thereon, including the imprisonment of Debs and his associates, were fully approved.

Thus the Supreme Court of the United States has written the closing words of this history, tragical in many of its details, and in every line provoking sober reflection. As we gratefully turn its concluding page, those who were most nearly related by executive responsibility to the troublous days whose story is told may well especially congratulate themselves on the part which fell to them in marking out the way and clearing the path, now unchangeably established, which shall hereafter guide our nation safely and surely in the exercise of the important functions which represent the people's trust.

THE BOND ISSUES

I

The sales of United States bonds in the years 1894, 1895, and 1896 for the purpose of replenishing the stock of gold in the public Treasury have been greatly misunderstood by many honest people, and often deliberately misrepresented.

My conviction that a love of fairness still abides with the masses of our people has encouraged me to give a history of these transactions for the benefit of those who are uninformed or have been misled concerning them. In undertaking this task I shall attempt to avoid unprofitable and tiresome explanation; but I shall, nevertheless, indulge in the recital of details to such an extent as may appear necessary to an easy understanding of the matter in hand. I desire, above all things, to treat the subject in such a way that none who read my narrative will be confused by the use of obscure or technical language.

The Government's gold reserve, as it is usually known, originated under the provision of an act of Congress passed January 14, 1875, entitled, "An Act to provide for the resumption of specie payments." This law contemplated the redemption in gold and the retirement of the currency obligations legally known as United States notes, but commonly called greenbacks; and it provided that such notes in excess of $300,000,000 should be redeemed and retired prior to January 1, 1879, and that after that date all the remainder of such notes should be likewise redeemed and canceled. This law further provided that "to enable the Secretary of the Treasury to prepare and provide for such redemption" he should have the authority "to issue, sell and dispose of" bonds of the United States which were therein particularly specified. Of course this authority was given to the Secretary of the Treasury in order that, by the sale of Government bonds, he could accumulate a sufficient gold fund or reserve to meet the demands of the gold redemption provided for, and accomplish the ultimate retirement of all the United States notes in circulation.

In compliance with this act, the sum of about $92,000,000 in gold was realized by the sale of bonds, and about $41,000,000, in addition, was obtained from surplus revenue; and thereupon the contemplated redemption was entered upon. But after the retirement and cancelation of only about $30,000,000 of these notes, and on the thirty-first day of May,

1878, this process was interrupted by the passage of an act forbidding their further retirement or cancelation, and providing that any such notes thereafter redeemed should not be canceled or destroyed, but should be "reissued and paid out again and kept in circulation." At the time this act was passed the United States notes uncanceled and still outstanding amounted to $346,681,016. It will be observed that though the actual retirement of these notes was prohibited, their redemption in gold was still continued, coupled with the condition that, though thus redeemed, they should be still kept on foot and again put in circulation as a continuing and never-ending obligation of the Government, calling for payment in gold— not once alone, but as often as their reissue permitted, and without the least regard to prior so-called redemptions. It will be also observed that this prohibition of cancelation intervened seven months prior to January 1, 1879, the date when the general and unrestricted redemption and retirement of all these outstanding notes was, under the terms of the act of 1875, to commence. At the time when their further cancelation was thus terminated there remained of the gold which had been provided as a reserve for their redemption about $103,000,000. This is the fund which has since then been called the "gold reserve."

In point of fact, this reserve was thereafter made up of all the net gold held by the Government; and its amount at any particular date was ascertained by deducting from the entire stock of gold in the Treasury the amounts covered by outstanding gold certificates, which instruments resemble a bank's certificate of deposit, and are issued by the Secretary of the Treasury to those making with the Government specific deposits of gold, to be returned to the holders of the certificates on demand. Of course the gold thus held for certificate-holders is not available for the redemption of United States notes.

In the year 1882 a law was passed by Congress which provided that the Secretary of the Treasury should suspend the issue of these gold certificates "whenever the amount of gold coin and gold bullion in the Treasury, reserved for the redemption of United States notes, falls below $100,000,000." Whatever may have been the actual relationship between gold certificates representing gold deposited for their redemption, and the gold kept on hand for the redemption of United States notes, the provision of law just quoted seems to have been accepted as a statutory recognition of the fact that our gold reserve for note redemption should have for its lowest limit this sum of $100,000,000. It is a singular circumstance that until very lately, when this reserve was increased and fixed at $150,000,000, no Act of Congress actually provided, or in any way expressly stated, what the limits of this gold reserve for redemption purposes should be; and it is no less singular that this provision in the law of 1882 fixed its lowest safe limit as perfectly and authoritatively in the understanding of our people as it could have been done by a distinct legislative requirement. At the time this reserve was created, as well as when the actual cancelation of United States notes after redemption was prohibited, it evidently was thought by those directing our nation's financial affairs that the sum of $100,000,000 in net gold actually in hand, especially with such additions as might naturally be expected to reach the fund by way of surplus revenue receipts, or otherwise, would constitute a sufficient gold reserve to redeem such of these notes still left outstanding as might be presented, and that the assurance of their gold redemption when presented would keep them largely in circulation. This scheme seemed for a time to be abundantly vindicated by the people's contentment with the sufficiency of the redemption reserve, and by their willingness to keep in circulating use these United States notes as currency more convenient than gold itself.

Another most important condition of mind among the people, however, grew out of, or at least accompanied, their acceptance of the redemptive sufficiency of the gold reserve as constituted. The popular belief became deep-seated and apparently immovable that the reduction of this gold reserve to an amount less than $100,000,000 would, in some way, cause a disastrous situation, and perhaps justify an apprehension concerning our nation's financial soundness. Thus a gold reserve containing at all times at least $100,000,000 came to be regarded by the people with a sort of sentimental solicitude, which, whatever else may be said of it, was certainly something to be reckoned with in making our national financial calculations.

That the plans thus set on foot for the so-called redemption of the United States notes outstanding promised to be adequate and effective is seen in the fact that the gold reserve, starting at the end of June, 1878, with about $103,500,000, never afterward fell as low as $100,000,000 until April, 1893, and that sometimes in its fluctuations during this interval of twenty-five years it amounted to upward of $200,000,000. Under conditions then existing popular confidence was well established, the reserve satisfactorily endured the strain of all redemption demands, and United States notes were kept well in circulation as money.

In an evil hour, however, a legislative concession was made to a mischievous and persistent demand for the free and unlimited coinage of silver. This concession was first exhibited in an act of Congress passed in 1878, directing the expenditure of not less than $2,000,000 nor more than $4,000,000 each month by the Secretary of the Treasury in the purchase of silver bullion, and the coinage of such bullion into silver dollars. Though this act is not in itself so intimately related to my subject as to require detailed explanation, it was the forerunner of another law of Congress which had much to do with creating the financial conditions that necessitated the issuance of Government bonds for the reinforcement of the gold reserve.

This law was passed in 1890, and superseded the provision of the law of 1878 directing the purchase and coinage of silver. In lieu of these provisions the Secretary of the Treasury was thereby directed to purchase silver bullion from time to time in each month to the aggregate amount of 4,500,000 ounces, or as much as might be offered, at the market price, not to exceed, however, a limit therein fixed. It was further provided that there should be issued, in payment of such purchases of silver bullion, Treasury notes of the United States in denominations not less than one dollar nor more than $1000; that such notes should be redeemable in coin, and should "be a legal tender in payment of all debts, public and private, except where otherwise expressly stipulated in the contract, and should be receivable for customs, taxes and all public dues"; and that when they were redeemed or paid into the Treasury they might be reissued. The Secretary of the Treasury was directed to coin into silver dollars in each month until the first day of July, 1891, 2,000,000 ounces of the silver so purchased, and thereafter so much as might be necessary to provide for the redemption of the notes issued in payment for the silver from time to time purchased under the act.

I have recited these provisions by way of leading up to the proposition that, under the law of 1890, the burden upon the gold reserve was tremendously enlarged. It will be readily seen that it forced larger monthly purchases of silver than were required under the prior act, and that, instead of providing for silver dollars, which as coins, or certificates of deposit representing such coins, should circulate as silver currency, unredeemable in gold as was done under the act of 1878, it directed that in payment of such purchases a new obligation of the Government, redeemable in coin, should be issued and added to our circulating medium.

It is, however, only when we examine the specific provision for the redemption of these notes that we discover in its full extent the harmful relationship of this new device to the integrity of the gold reserve. At its outset the redemption clause of the act courageously and manfully gave to the Secretary of the Treasury the authority to redeem such notes in gold or silver *at his discretion*; but in its ending it fell down a pitiful victim of the silver craze. The entire clause is in these words: "That upon demand of the holder of any of the Treasury notes herein provided for, the Secretary of the Treasury shall, under such regulations as he may provide, redeem such notes in gold or silver coin at his discretion, *it being the established policy of the United States to maintain the two metals at a parity with each other upon the present legal ratio, or such ratio as may be provided by law.*"

According to the legal ratio then existing, which has never been changed, the average intrinsic gold value of a silver dollar as compared with a gold dollar was, during the year 1891, about seventy-six cents, during 1892 a trifle more than sixty-seven cents, and during 1893 about sixty cents.

It is hardly necessary to say that the assertion in the act of "the established policy of the United States to maintain the two metals at a parity" had the effect of transferring the discretion of determining whether these Treasury notes should be redeemed in gold or silver, from the Secretary of the Treasury to the holder of the notes. Manifestly, in the face of this assertion of the Government's intention, a demand for gold redemption on the part of the holders of such notes could not be refused, and the acceptance of silver dollars insisted upon, without either subjecting to doubt the good faith and honest intention of the Government's professions, or creating a suspicion of our country's solvency. The parity between the two metals could not be maintained, but, on the contrary, would be distinctly denied, if the Secretary of the Treasury persisted in redeeming these notes, against the will of the holders, in dollars of silver instead of gold.

Therefore it came to pass that the Treasury notes issued for the purchase of silver under the law of 1890 took their place by the side of the United States notes, commonly called greenbacks, as demands against our very moderate and shifting gold reserve.

It should have been plainly apparent to all who had eyes to see that the monetary scheme, thus additionally burdened, was adequate and safe only in smooth financial weather, and was miserably calculated to resist any disturbances in public confidence, or the rough waves of business emergencies. The proof of this was quickly forthcoming.

The new Treasury notes made their first appearance as part of our money circulation in August, 1890; and at the close of that month the gold reserve amounted to $185,837,581. During the next month it fell off about $38,000,000, reducing the amount on the last day of September to nearly $148,000,000; and with a few slight spasmodic rallies it continued to decrease until the sale of bonds for its replenishment.

In the latter part of 1892 and the first months of 1893, these Treasury notes having, in the meantime, very greatly multiplied, the withdrawals of gold from the Treasury through the redemption of these as well as the United States notes strikingly increased; and the fact that by far the larger part of the gold so withdrawn was shipped abroad plainly showed that foreign investors in American securities had grave apprehensions as to our ability to continue to redeem all these notes in gold and thus maintain the integrity and soundness of our financial condition.

I succeeded Mr. Harrison in the Presidency on the fourth day of March, 1893; and on the seventh of that month Mr. Carlisle became Secretary of the Treasury. The gold reserve on that day amounted to $100,982,410— only $982,410 in excess of the sum that had come to be generally regarded as indicating the danger line. The retiring Secretary of the Treasury, appreciating the importance of preventing the fall of the reserve below this limit, had just before his retirement directed the preparation of plates for the engraving of bonds so that he might by their sale obtain gold to reinforce the fund. I have heard him say within the last few years that he expected before the close of his term to resort to bond sales for the purpose of such reinforcement, unless prevented at the last moment by the President's disapproval. Of course it is but natural that any one directing the affairs of the Treasury Department should be anxious to avoid such an expedient; and Secretary Foster avoided it, and barely saved the reserve from falling below the $100,000,000 mark during his term, by effecting arrangements, in January and February, 1893, with certain bankers in New York, by which he obtained from them in exchange for United States notes, or on other considerations, something over $8,000,000 in gold, which enabled him to escape the sale of bonds in aid of the reserve.

With the gold reserve lower than it had ever been since its creation in 1878, and showing an excess of less than $1,000,000 above the supposed limit of disaster, and with the demand for gold redemption of Government currency obligations giving no sign of abatement, the prospect that greeted the new administration was certainly not reassuring. In our effort to meet the emergency without an issue of bonds Secretary Carlisle immediately applied to banks in different localities for an exchange with the Government of a portion of their holdings of gold coin for other forms of currency. This effort was so far successful that on the 25th of March the gold reserve amounted to over $107,000,000, notwithstanding the fact that considerable withdrawals had been made in the interval. The slight betterment thus secured proved, however, to be only temporary; for under the stress of continued and augmented withdrawals, the gold reserve, on the twenty-second day of April, 1893, for the first time since its establishment, was reduced below the $100,000,000 limit—amounting on that day to about $97,000,000.

Though this fall below the minimum theretofore always maintained was not followed by any sudden and distinctly new disaster, it had the effect of accelerating withdrawals of gold. It became apparent that there had intervened a growing apprehension among the masses of our own people concerning the Government's competency to continue gold redemption, with the result that a greatly increased proportion of the amount withdrawn from the gold reserve, instead of going abroad to satisfy the claims of foreigners or as a basis of commercial exchange, was hoarded by our citizens at home as a precaution against possible financial distress. In the meantime, nearly the entire gold receipts in payment of customs and other revenue charges had ceased. To meet this situation strenuous efforts were made by the Secretary of the Treasury to improve the condition by resorting again to the plan of exchanging for gold other forms of currency, with some success, while in the month of August, 1893, gold revenue receipts were temporarily considerably stimulated. Thus a fleeting gleam of hope was given to the dark surroundings.

In these troublous times those charged with the administration of the Government's financial affairs could not fail to recognize in the law of 1890, directing the monthly purchase of silver and the issuance in payment therefor of Treasury notes in effect redeemable in gold, a prolific cause of our financial trouble. Accordingly, a special session of Congress was called to meet on the seventh day of August, 1893, to repeal this law, and thus terminate the creation of further demands upon our already overburdened and feeble gold reserve. The repealing act was quite promptly passed in the House of Representatives on the twenty-eighth day of August; but, on account of vexatious opposition in the Senate, the repeal was not finally effected until the first day of November, 1893, and then only after there had been added to the act an inopportune repetition of the statement concerning the Government's intention to maintain the parity of both gold and silver coins.

II

The effect of this repeal in its immediate results failed to quiet the fear of impending evil now thoroughly aroused; nor were all the efforts thus far made to augment the gold reserve effective as against the constant process of its depletion.

On the seventeenth day of January, 1894, the Government was confronted by a disquieting emergency. The gold reserve had fallen to less than $70,000,000, notwithstanding the most diligent efforts to maintain it in sounder condition. Against this slender fund gold demands amounting to not less than $450,000,000 in United States notes and Treasury notes were in actual circulation, and others amounting to about $50,000,000, in addition, were temporarily held in the Treasury subject to reissue—the entire volume, by peremptory requirement of law, remaining uncanceled even after repeated redemption; nor was there any promise of a cessation of the abnormal and exhausting drain of gold then fully under way. Another factor in the situation, most perplexing and dangerous, was the distrust, which was growing enormously, regarding the wisdom and stability of our scheme of finance. As a result of these conditions there loomed in sight the menace of the destruction of our gold reserve, the repudiation of our gold obligations, the humiliating fall of our nation's finances to a silver basis, and the degradation of our Government's high standing in the respect of the civilized world.

There was absolutely but one way to avert national calamity and our country's disgrace; and this way was adopted when, on the seventeenth day of January, 1894, the Secretary of the Treasury issued a notice that bids in gold would be received until the first day of February following for $50,000,000 in bonds of the United States, redeemable in coin at the pleasure of the Government after ten years from the date of their issue, and bearing interest at the rate of five per cent. per annum. It was further stated in the notice that no bid would be considered that did not offer a premium on said bonds of a fraction more than seventeen per cent., which would secure to the purchaser an investment yielding three per cent. per annum.

It should here be mentioned that the only Government bonds which could be sold in the manner and for the purpose contemplated were such as were authorized and described in a law passed in 1870, and which were designated in the law of 1875 providing for the redemption of United States notes as the kind of bonds which the Secretary of the Treasury was permitted to sell to enable him "to prepare and provide for" such redemption. The issues of bonds thus authorized were of three descriptions: one payable at the pleasure of the Government after ten years from their date, and bearing interest at the rate of five per cent.; one so made payable after fifteen years from their date, bearing four and a half per cent. interest; and one in like manner made payable after thirty years from their date, bearing interest at the rate of four per cent. The five per cent. bonds were specified in the Secretary's offer of sale because on account of their high rate of interest they would command a greater premium, and therefore a larger return of gold, and for the further reason that the option of the Government regarding their payment could be earlier exercised.

The withdrawals of gold did not cease with the offer to sell bonds for the replenishment of the reserve, and on the day before the date limited for the opening of bids the fund had decreased to less than $66,000,000. In the meantime, the perplexity of the situation, already intense, was made more so by the fact that the bids for bonds under the offer of the Secretary came in so slowly that a few days before the 1st of February, when the bids were to be opened, there were plain indications that the contemplated sale would fail unless prompt and energetic measures were taken to avoid such a perilous result.

Thereupon the Secretary of the Treasury invited to a conference, in the city of New York, a number of bankers and presidents of moneyed institutions, which resulted in so arousing their patriotism, as well as their solicitude for the protection of the interests they represented, that they effectively exerted themselves, barely in time to prevent a disastrous failure of the sale. The proceeds of this sale, received from numerous bidders large and small, aggregated $58,660,917.63 in gold, which so increased the reserve that on the sixth day of March, 1894, it amounted to $107,440,802.

It was hoped that this measure of restoration and this exhibition of the nation's ability to protect its financial integrity would allay apprehension and restore confidence to such an extent as to render further bond sales unnecessary. It was soon discovered, however, that the complications of our ill condition were so deep-seated and stubborn that the treatment resorted to was only a palliative instead of a cure.

On the last day of May, 1894, less than three months after its reinforcement, as mentioned, the gold reserve had been again so depleted by withdrawals that it amounted to only $78,693,267. An almost uninterrupted downward tendency followed, notwithstanding constant efforts on the part of the Government to check the fall, until, on the fourteenth day of November, 1894, the fund had fallen to $61,878,374. In the meantime, the inclination of our timid citizens to take gold from the reserve for hoarding "had grown by what it fed on," while large shipments abroad to meet foreign indebtedness or for profit still continued and increased in amount.

In these circumstances the inexorable alternative presented itself of again selling Government bonds for the replenishment of its redemption gold, or assuming the tremendous risk of neglecting the safety and permanence of every interest dependent upon the soundness of our national finances. An obedient regard for official duty made the right path exceedingly plain.

On the day last mentioned a public proposal was issued inviting bids in gold for the purchase of additional five per cent. bonds to the amount of $50,000,000. Numerous bids were received under this proposal, one of which, for "all or none" of the bonds, tendered on behalf of thirty-three banking institutions and financiers in the city of New York, being considerably more advantageous to the Government than all other bids, was accepted, and the entire amount was awarded to these parties. This resulted in adding to the reserve the sum of $58,538,500.

The president at that time of the United States Trust Company, one of the strongest and largest financial institutions in the country, rendered most useful and patriotic service in making both this and the previous offer of bonds successful; and his company was a prominent purchaser on both occasions. He afterward testified under oath that the accepted bid for "all or none," in which his company was a large participant, proved unprofitable to the bidders.

The payment of gold into the Treasury on account of this sale of bonds was not entirely completed until after the 1st of December, 1894. Then followed a time of bitter disappointment and miserable depression, greater than any that had before darkened the struggles of the Executive branch of the Government to save our nation's financial integrity.

The addition made to the gold reserve by this completed transaction seemed to be of no substantial benefit, if, on the contrary, it did not actually stimulate the disquieting factors of the situation. In December, 1894, during which month $58,538,500 in gold, realized from this second sale of bonds, was fully paid in and added to the reserve, the withdrawals from the fund amounted to nearly $32,000,000; and this was followed in the next month, or during January, 1895, by a further depletion in the sum of more than $45,000,000.

In view of the crisis which these suddenly increased withdrawals seemed to portend, the aid of Congress was earnestly invoked in a special presidential message to that body, dated on the 28th of January, 1895, in which the gravity and embarrassment of the situation were set forth in the following terms:

> The real trouble which confronts us consists in a lack of confidence, widespread and constantly increasing, in the continuing ability or disposition of the Government to pay its obligations in gold. This lack of confidence grows to some extent out of the palpable and apparent embarrassment attending the efforts of the Government under existing laws to procure gold, and to a greater extent out of the impossibility of either keeping it in the Treasury or canceling obligations by its expenditure after it is obtained....

> The most dangerous and irritating feature of the situation, however, remains to be mentioned. It is found in the means by which the Treasury is despoiled of the gold thus obtained (by the sale of bonds) without canceling a single Government obligation, and solely for the benefit of those who find profit in shipping it abroad, or whose fears induce them to hoard it at home. We have outstanding about $500,000,000 of currency notes of the Government for which gold may be demanded, and, curiously enough, the law requires that when presented, and, in fact,

redeemed and paid in gold, they shall be reissued. Thus the same notes may do duty many times in drawing gold from the Treasury; nor can the process be averted so long as private parties, for profit or otherwise, see an advantage in repeating the operation. More than $300,000,000 of these notes have been redeemed in gold, and, notwithstanding such redemption, they are still outstanding.

After giving a history of the bond issues already made to replenish the reserve, and of their results, it was further stated:

The financial events of the past year suggest facts and conditions which should certainly arrest attention. More than $172,000,000 in gold have been drawn out of the Treasury during the year for the purpose of shipment abroad or hoarding at home.

While nearly $103,000,000 was drawn out during the first ten months of the year, a sum aggregating more than two-thirds of that amount, being about $69,000,000, was drawn out during the following two months, thus indicating a marked acceleration of the depleting process with the lapse of time.

Following a reference to existing differences of opinion in regard to the extent to which silver should be coined or used in our currency, and the irrelevancy of such differences to the matter in hand, the message continued:

While I am not unfriendly to silver, and while I desire to see it recognized to such an extent as is consistent with financial safety and the preservation of national honor and credit, I am not willing to see gold entirely banished from our currency and finances. To avert such a consequence I believe thorough and radical remedial legislation should be promptly passed. I therefore beg the Congress to give the subject immediate attention.

After recommending the passage of a law authorizing the issue of long-term bonds, bearing a low rate of interest, to be used for the maintenance of an adequate gold reserve and in exchange for outstanding United States notes and Treasury notes for the purpose of their cancelation, and after giving details of the proposed scheme, the message concluded as follows:

In conclusion, I desire to frankly confess my reluctance to issue more bonds in present circumstances and with no better results than have lately followed that course. I cannot, however, refrain from adding to an assurance of my anxiety to co-operate with the present Congress in any reasonable measure of relief, an expression of my determination to leave nothing undone which furnishes a hope for improving the situation, or checking a suspicion of our disinclination or disability to meet, with the strictest honor, every national obligation.

This appeal to Congress for legislative aid was absolutely fruitless.

On the eighth day of February, 1895, those who, under the mandate of Executive duty, were striving, thus unaided, to avert the perils of the situation, could count in the gold reserve only the frightfully low sum of $41,340,181; and it must be remembered that this was only two months after the proceeds of the second sale of bonds had been added to the fund. In point of fact, the withdrawals of gold during the short period mentioned had exceeded by more than $18,000,000 the amount of such proceeds; and several million dollars more had been demanded, some of which, though actually taken out, was unexpectedly, and on account of the transaction now to be detailed, returned to the Treasury.

This sudden fall in the reserve, and the apparent certainty of the continuance of its rapid depletion, seemed to justify the fear that before another bond sale by means of public notice and popular subscription could be perfected the gold reserve might be entirely exhausted; nor could we keep out of mind the apprehension that in consequence of repeated dispositions of bonds, with worse instead of better financial conditions impending, further sales by popular subscription might fail of success, except upon terms that would give the appearance of impaired national credit.

Notwithstanding all this, no other way seemed to be open to us than another public offer of bonds; and it was determined to move in that direction immediately.

In anticipation of this action it was important to obtain certain information and suggestions touching the feeling and disposition of those actively prominent in financial and business circles.

I think it may here be frankly confessed that it never occurred to any of us to consult, in this emergency, farmers, doctors, lawyers, shoe-makers, or even statesmen. We could not escape the belief that the prospect of obtaining what we needed might be somewhat improved by making application to those whose business and surroundings qualified them to intelligently respond.

Therefore, on the evening of the seventh day of February, 1895, an interview was held at the White House with Mr. J. P. Morgan of New York; and I propose to give the details of that interview as gathered from a recollection which I do not believe can be at fault. Secretary Carlisle was present nearly or quite all the time, Attorney-General Olney was there a portion of the time, and Mr. Morgan and a young man from his office and myself all the time. At the outset Mr. Morgan was inclined to complain of the treatment he had received from Treasury officials in the repudiation of an arrangement which he thought he had been encouraged to perfect in connection with the disposal of another issue of bonds. I said to Mr. Morgan, whatever there might be in all this, another offer of bonds for popular subscription open to all bidders had been determined upon, and that there were two questions I wanted to ask him which he ought to be able to answer: one was whether the bonds to be so offered would probably be taken at a good price on short notice; and the other was whether, in case there should be imminent danger of the disappearance of what remained of the gold reserve, during the time that must elapse between published notice and the opening of bids, a sufficient amount of gold could be temporarily obtained from financial institutions in the city of New York to bridge over the difficulty and save the reserve until the Government could realize upon the sale of its bonds. Mr. Morgan replied that he had no doubt bonds could be again sold on popular subscription at some price, but he could not say what the price would be; and to the second inquiry his answer was that, in his opinion, such an advance of gold as might be required could be accomplished if the gold could be kept in this country, but that there might be reluctance to making such an advance if it was to be immediately withdrawn for shipment abroad, leaving our financial condition substantially unimproved. After a little further discussion of the situation he suddenly asked me why we did not buy $100,000,000 in gold at a fixed price and pay for it in bonds, under Section 3700 of the Revised Statutes. This was a proposition entirely new to me. I turned to the Statutes and read the section he had mentioned. Secretary Carlisle confirmed me in the opinion that this law abundantly authorized such a transaction, and agreed that it might be expedient if favorable terms could be made. The section of the Statutes referred to reads as follows:

> *Section 3700.* The Secretary of the Treasury may purchase coin with any of the bonds or notes of the United States authorized by law, at such rates and upon such terms as he may deem most advantageous to the public interest.

Mr. Morgan strongly urged that, if we proceeded under this law, the amount of gold purchased should not be less than $100,000,000; but he was at once informed that in no event would more bonds be then issued than would be sufficient to provide for adding to the reserve, about $60,000,000, the amount necessary to raise the fund to $100,000,000.

Not many months afterward I became convinced that on this point Mr. Morgan made a wise suggestion; and I have always since regretted that it was not adopted.

III

It can hardly be necessary to state that any plan which would protect from immediate withdrawal the gold we might add to our reserve could not fail to be of extreme value. Such of these withdrawals as were made for hoarding gold could be prevented only by a restoration of confidence among those of our people who had grown suspicious of the Government's financial ability; but the considerable drain from the reserve for the purchase of the very bonds to be sold for its reinforcement, and the much larger drain made by those who profited by the shipment of gold abroad, could be, measurably at least, directly arrested. Thus to the extent that foreign gold might be brought here and used for the purchase of bonds, the use for that purpose of such as was held by our own people or as was already in the reserve subject to their withdrawal would not only be decreased, but the current of the passage of gold would be changed and would flow toward us instead of away from us, making the prospect of profit in gold exportation less alluring. An influx of gold from abroad would also have a tendency to decrease the sentimental estimate of its desirability which its unrelieved scarcity was apt to create in timid minds. It was especially plain that so far as withdrawals from our reserve for speculative shipment abroad were concerned, they could be discouraged by the efforts of those whose financial connections in other countries enabled them to sell gold exchange on foreign money centers at a price which would make the actual transportation of the coin itself unprofitable.

The position of Mr. Morgan and the other parties in interest whom he represented was such in the business world that they were abundantly able, not only to furnish the gold we needed, but to protect us in the manner indicated against its immediate loss. Their willingness to undertake both these services was developed during the discussion of the plan proposed; and after careful consideration of every detail until a late hour of the night, an agreement was made by which J. P. Morgan & Co. of New York, for themselves and for J. S. Morgan & Co. of London; and August Belmont & Co. of New York, for themselves and for N. M. Rothschild & Son of London, were to sell and deliver to the Government 3,500,000 ounces of standard gold coin of the United States, to be paid for in bonds bearing annual interest at the rate of four per cent. per annum, and payable at the pleasure of the Government after thirty years from their date, such bonds to be issued and delivered from time to time as the gold coin to be furnished was deposited by said parties in the subtreasuries or other legal depositories of the United States. At least one half of the coin so delivered was to be obtained in Europe, and shipped from there in amounts not less than 300,000 ounces per month, at the expense and risk of the parties furnishing the same; and so far as it was in their power they were to "exert all financial influence and make all legitimate efforts to protect the Treasury of the United States against the withdrawals of gold pending the complete performance of the contract."

Four per cent. bonds were selected for use in this transaction instead of ten-year bonds bearing five per cent. interest, because their maturity was extended to thirty years, thus offering a more permanent and inviting investment, and for the further reason that $100,000,000 of shorter five per cent. bonds had already been issued, and it was, therefore, deemed desirable to postpone these further bond obligations of the Government to a later date. The price agreed upon for the gold coin to be delivered was such that the bonds given in payment therefor would yield to the investor an annual income of three and three fourths per cent.

It has already been stated that the only bonds which could be utilized in our efforts to maintain our gold reserve were those described in a law passed as early as 1870, and made available for our uses by an act passed in 1875. The terms of these bonds were ill suited to later ideas of investment, and they were made payable in coin and not specifically in gold. Nothing at any time induced the exchange of gold for these coin bonds, except a reliance upon such a measure of good faith on the part of the Government, and honesty on the part of the people, as would assure their payment in gold coin and not in depreciated silver.

It was exceedingly fortunate that, at the time this agreement was under consideration, certain political movements calculated to undermine this reliance upon the Government's continued financial integrity were not in sight; but it was, nevertheless, very apparent that the difficulties of the situation would be greatly lessened if, in safeguarding our reserve, bonds could be used payable by their terms in gold, and bearing a rate of interest not exceeding three per cent. Accordingly, at the instance of Secretary Carlisle, a bill had been introduced in the House of Representatives, some time before the Morgan-Belmont agreement was entered upon, which authorized the issue of bonds of that description. A few hours before the agreement was consummated this sane and sensible legislation was brought to a vote in the House and rejected.

When, in our interview with Mr. Morgan, the price for the gold to be furnished was considered, he gave reasons which we could not well answer in support of the terms finally agreed upon; but he said that the parties offering to furnish the gold would be glad to accept at par three per cent. bonds, payable by their terms in gold instead of in coin, in case their issue could be authorized. He expressed not only a willingness but a strong desire that a substitution might be made of such bonds in lieu of those already selected, and readily agreed to allow us time to procure the necessary legislation for that purpose. He explained, however, that only a short time could be stipulated for such a substitution, because in order to carry out successfully the agreement contemplated, the bonds must be offered in advance to investors both here and abroad, and that after numerous subscriptions had been received from outside parties the form and condition of the securities could not be changed; and he added that, but for this, there would be no objection to the concession of all the time desired. It was finally agreed that ten days should be allowed us to secure from Congress the legislation necessary to permit the desired substitution of bonds. A simple calculation demonstrated that by such a substitution the Government would save on account of interest more than $16,000,000 before the maturity of the bonds. It was further stipulated on the part of the Government that if the Secretary of the Treasury should desire to sell any further bonds on or before October 1, 1895, they should first be offered to the parties then represented by Mr. Morgan. This stipulation did not become operative.

When our conference terminated it was understood that Secretary Carlisle and Attorney-General Olney should act for the Government at a meeting between the parties early the following day, at which the agreement we had made was to be reduced to writing; and thereupon I prepared a message which was submitted to the Congress at the opening of its session on the following day, in which the details of our agreement were set forth and the amount which would be saved to the Government by the substitution of three per cent. gold bonds was plainly stated; but having no memorandum of the agreement before me, in my haste I carelessly omitted to mention the efforts agreed on by Mr. Morgan and his associates to prevent gold shipments. The next morning a contract embodying our agreement was drawn and signed, and a copy at once given to the chairman of the Ways and Means Committee of the House, so that the delay of a demand for its inspection might be avoided. A bill was also immediately introduced again giving authority to issue three per cent. bonds, payable by their terms in gold, to be substituted in place of the four per cent. bonds as provided in the contract—to the end that $16,000,000 might be saved to the Government, and the public welfare in every way subserved.

The object of this message was twofold. It was deemed important, considering the critical condition of our gold reserve, that the public should be speedily informed of the steps taken for its protection; and in addition, though previous efforts to obtain helpful legislation had resulted in discouragement, it was hoped that when the saving by the Government of $16,000,000 was seen to depend on the action of Congress there might be a response that would accord with patriotic public duty.

Quite in keeping with the congressional habit prevailing at that time, the needed legislation was refused, and this money was not saved.

The contract was thereupon carried out as originally made. In its execution four per cent. bonds were delivered amounting to $62,315,400, and the sum of $65,116,244.62 in gold received as their price. The last deposit in completion of the contract was made in June, 1895, but additional gold was obtained from the contracting parties in exchange for United States notes and Treasury notes until in September, 1895, when the entire amount of gold received from them under the contract and through such exchanges had amounted to more than $81,000,000. The terms of the agreement were so well carried out, not only in the matter of furnishing gold, but in procuring it from abroad and protecting the reserve from withdrawals, that during its continuance the operation of the "endless chain" which had theretofore drained our gold was interrupted. No gold was, during that period, taken from the Treasury to be used in the purchase of bonds, as had previously been the case, nor was any withdrawn for shipment abroad.

It became manifest, however, soon after this contract was fully performed, that our financial ailments had reached a stage so nearly chronic that their cure by any treatment within Executive reach might well be considered a matter of anxious doubt. In the latter months of the year 1895 a scarcity of foreign exchange and its high rate, the termination of the safeguards of the Morgan-Belmont contract, and, as a result, the renewal of opportunity profitably to withdraw gold for export with a newly stimulated popular apprehension, and perhaps other disturbing incidents, brought about a recurrence of serious depletions of gold from the reserve.

In the annual Executive message sent to Congress on the second day of December, 1895, the situation of our finances and currency was set forth in detail, and another earnest plea was made for remedial legislative action. After mentioning the immediately satisfactory results of the contract for the purchase of gold, the message continued:

> Though the contract mentioned stayed for a time the tide of gold withdrawals, its good results could not be permanent. Recent withdrawals have reduced the reserve from $107,571,230 on the eighth day of July, 1895, to

$79,333,966. How long it will remain large enough to render its increase unnecessary is only a matter of conjecture, though quite large withdrawals for shipment in the immediate future are predicted in well-informed quarters. About $16,000,000 has been withdrawn during the month of November.

The prediction of further withdrawals mentioned in this message was so fully verified that eighteen days after its transmission, and on the twentieth day of December, 1895, another Executive communication was sent to Congress, in contemplation of its holiday recess, in which, after referring to the details contained in the former message, it was stated:

The contingency then feared has reached us, and the withdrawals of gold since the communication referred to, and others that appear inevitable, threaten such a depletion in our Government's gold reserve as brings us face to face with the necessity of further action for its protection. This condition is intensified by the prevalence in certain quarters of sudden and unusual apprehension and timidity in business circles.

The real and sensible cure for our recurring troubles can only be effected by a complete change in our financial scheme. Pending that, the Executive branch of the Government will not relax its efforts nor abandon its determination to use every means within its reach to maintain before the world American credit, nor will there be any hesitation in exhibiting its confidence in the resources of our country and the constant patriotism of our people.

In view, however, of the peculiar situation now confronting us, I have ventured to herein express the earnest hope that the Congress, in default of the inauguration of a better system of finance, will not take a recess from its labors before it has, by legislative enactment or declaration, done something, not only to remind those apprehensive among our own people that the resources of this Government and a scrupulous regard for honest dealing afford a sure guarantee of unquestioned safety and soundness, but to reassure the world that with these factors, and the patriotism of our citizens, the ability and determination of our nation to meet in any circumstances every obligation it incurs do not admit of question.

Perhaps it should not have been expected that members of Congress would permit troublesome thoughts of the Government's financial difficulties to disturb the pleasant anticipations of their holiday recess; at any rate, these difficulties and the appeal of the President for at least some manifestation of a disposition to aid in their remedy were completely ignored.

On the sixth day of January, 1896, the gold reserve having fallen to $61,251,710, its immediate repair became imperative. Though our resort to the expedient of purchasing gold with bonds under contract had been productive of very satisfactory results, it by no means indicated our abandonment of the policy of inviting offerings of gold by public advertisement. It was rather an exceptional departure from that policy, made necessary by the dangerously low state of the reserve on account of extensive and sudden depletions, and the peril attending any delay in replenishing it. We had not lost faith in the loyalty and patriotism of the people, nor did we doubt their willingness to respond to an appeal from their Government in any emergency. We also confidently believed that if the bonds issued for the purpose of increasing our stock of gold were widely distributed among our people, self-interest as well as patriotism would stimulate the solicitude of the masses of our citizens for the welfare of the nation. No reason for discouragement had been found in public offerings for bonds, so far as obtaining a needed supply of gold and a fair price for our bonds were concerned. The failure of their wide distribution among the people when so disposed of seemed to be largely owing to the fact that the bonds themselves were so antiquated in form, and bore so high a rate of interest, that it was difficult for an ordinary person to make the rather confusing computation of premium and other factors necessary to a safe and intelligent bid. In a transaction of this sort, where the smallest fraction of a cent may determine the success of an offer, those accustomed to the niceties of financial calculations are apt to hold the field to the exclusion of many who, unaided, dare not trust themselves in the haze of such intricacies. If Congress had provided for the issuance of bonds bearing a low rate of interest, which could have been offered to the public at par, I am convinced that the plain people of the land would more generally have become purchasers. Another difficulty that had to some extent prevented a more common participation by the people in prior public sales arose, it was thought, from their lack of notice of the pendency of such sales, and want of information as to the advantages of the investment offered, and the procedure necessary to present their bids in proper form.

In view of the fact that the gold then in the reserve amounted to $20,000,000 more than it contained eleven months earlier, when the Morgan-Belmont contract was made, and because, for that reason, more time could be allowed for its replenishment, there was no hesitation in deciding upon a return to our original plan of offering bonds in exchange for gold by public subscription.

Having determined upon a return to this method, it was deemed wise, upon consideration of all the circumstances, to make some modification of prior action in such cases. Instead of short-term five per cent. bonds, the longer-term bonds bearing four per cent. interest were substituted, as, on the whole, the best we could offer for popular subscription. Since two offerings of $50,000,000 each had proved to be of only very temporary benefit, it was determined to double the amount and offer $100,000,000 for subscription. Nearly a month was to be given instead of a shorter time, as theretofore, between the date of notice of the offer and the opening of the bids; and extraordinary efforts were to be made to give the most thorough publicity to the offerings—to the end that we might stimulate in every possible way the desire of the masses of our people to invest in the bonds. Especial information and aid were to be furnished for the guidance of those inclined to subscribe; and successful bidders were to be allowed to pay for the bonds awarded to them in instalments. The lowest denomination of the bonds was to be fifty dollars, and the larger ones were to be in multiples of that sum. In point of fact, it was resolved that nothing should be left undone which would in any way promote the success of this additional and increased offer of bond subscription to the public.

Accordingly, on the sixth day of January, 1896, a circular bearing that date was issued, giving notice that proposals would be received until the fifth day of February following for gold coin purchases of $100,000,000 of the four per cent. bonds of the United States, upon the terms above mentioned. These circulars were extensively published in the newspapers throughout the country. Copies, together with a letter of instruction to bidders, containing, among other things, a computation showing the income the bonds would yield to the investor upon their purchase at prices therein specified, and accompanied by blanks for subscription, were sent to the postmasters in every State and Territory with directions that they should be conspicuously displayed in their offices. The Comptroller of the Currency prepared and sent to all national banks a circular letter, urging them to call the attention of their patrons to the desirability of obtaining the bonds as an investment, and to aid in stimulating subscriptions; and with this was forwarded a complete set of papers similar to those sent to the postmasters. These papers were also sent to other banks and financial institutions and to bankers in all parts of the country, and, in addition, notice was given that they could be obtained upon application to the Treasury Department or any of the subtreasuries of the United States. Soon afterward, in view of the large amount of the bonds offered, and as a precaution against an undue strain upon the general money market, as well as to permit the greatest possible opportunity for subscription, the terms of the original offer of the Secretary of the Treasury were modified by reducing in amount the instalments of the purchase price and extending the time for their payment.

On an examination of the bids at the expiration of the time limited for their presentation, it was found that 4635 bids had been received, after rejecting six which were palpably not genuine or not made in good faith. The bidders were scattered through forty-seven of our States and Territories, and the aggregate amount represented by their bids was $526,970,000. The number of accepted bids upon which bonds were awarded was only 828, and of these ten were forfeited after acceptance, on account of non-payment of the first instalment of the purchase price. Several of the bids accepted were for a single fifty-dollar bond, and they varied in amount from that to one bid made by J. P. Morgan & Co. and several associates for the entire issue of $100,000,000, for which they offered 110.6877 on the dollar. To all the other 827 accepted bidders who offered even the smallest fraction of a farthing more than this the full number of bonds for which they bid were awarded.

The aggregate of the bonds awarded to these bidders, excluding the Morgan bid, amounted to $62,321,150. The remainder of the entire offering, including more than $4,700,000 of the awards which became forfeited for non-payment as above mentioned, were awarded to Mr. Morgan and his associates, their bid being the highest next to those on which bonds had been awarded in full, as already stated.

The aggregate of the prices received for these bonds represented, by reason of the premiums paid, an income to the investor of a trifle less than three and four tenths per cent.

As a result of this large sale of bonds, the gold reserve, which, on the last day of January, 1896, amounted to less than $50,000,000, was so increased that at the end of February, in spite of withdrawals in the meantime, it stood at nearly $124,000,000.

It will be observed that, notwithstanding all the efforts made to distribute this issue of bonds among the people, but 827 bids out of 4641 were entitled to awards as being above the Morgan bid; and that more than one third of all the bonds sold were awarded on the single bid of Mr. Morgan and his associates.

The price received on this public sale was apparently somewhat better for the Government than that secured by the Morgan-Belmont contract; but their agreement required of them such labor, risk, and expense as perhaps entitled them to a favorable bargain. In any event, the advantages the Government derived from this contract were certainly very valuable and should not be overlooked. On every sale of bonds by public offering, not excluding that just mentioned, large amounts of gold were withdrawn from the Treasury and used in paying for the bonds offered. In the execution of the contract of February, 1895, no gold was withdrawn for the purchase of the bonds, and the reserve received the full benefit of the transaction. Each sale by public advertisement made prior to the time of the contract had been so quickly followed by extensive and wasting withdrawals of gold from the reserve, that scarcely a breathing-time was allowed before we were again overtaken by the necessity for its reinforcement. Even after the notice given for the last sale on the eighth day of January, 1896, and between that date and the 1st of June following, these withdrawals amounted to more than $73,000,000, while during the six months or more of the existence of the Morgan-Belmont contract the withdrawals of gold for export were entirely prevented and a season of financial quiet and peace was secured.

Whatever may be the comparative merits of the two plans for maintaining our gold reserve, both of them when utilized were abundantly and clearly justified.

Whether from fatigue of malign conditions or other causes, ever since the last large sale of bonds was made the gold reserve has been so free from depletion that its condition has caused no alarm.

Two hundred and sixty-two millions of dollars in bonds were issued on its account during the critical time covered by this narrative; but the credit and fair fame of our nation were saved.

I have attempted to give a detailed history of the crime charged against an administration which "issued bonds of the Government in time of peace." Without shame and without repentance, I confess my share of the guilt; and I refuse to shield my accomplices in this crime who, with me, held high places in that administration. And though Mr. Morgan and Mr. Belmont and scores of other bankers and financiers who were accessories in these transactions may be steeped in destructive propensities, and may be constantly busy in sinful schemes, I shall always recall with satisfaction and self-congratulation my association with them at a time when our country sorely needed their aid.

THE VENEZUELAN BOUNDARY CONTROVERSY

I

There is no better illustration of the truth that nations and individuals are affected in the same manner by like causes than is often furnished by the beginning, progress, and results of a national boundary dispute. We all know that among individuals, when neighbors have entered upon a quarrel concerning their division-line or the location of a line fence, they will litigate until all account of cost and all regard for the merits of the contention give place to a ruthless and all-dominating determination, by fair means or foul, to win; and if fisticuffs and forcible possession are resorted to, the big, strong neighbor rejoices in his strength as he mauls and disfigures his small and weak antagonist.

It will be found that nations behave in like fashion. One or the other of two national neighbors claims that their dividing-line should be defined or rectified in a certain manner. If this is questioned, a season of diplomatic untruthfulness and finesse sometimes intervenes for the sake of appearances. Developments soon follow, however, that expose a grim determination behind fine phrases of diplomacy; and in the end the weaker nation frequently awakens to the fact that it must either accede to an ultimatum dictated by its stronger adversary, or look in the face of war and a spoliation of its territory; and if such a stage is reached, superior strength and fighting ability, instead of suggesting magnanimity, are graspingly used to enforce extreme demands if not to consummate extensive conquest or complete subjugation.

I propose to call attention to one of these unhappy national boundary disputes, between the kingdom of Great Britain and the South American republic of Venezuela, involving the boundary-line separating Venezuela from the English colony of British Guiana, which adjoins Venezuela on the east.

Venezuela, once a Spanish possession, declared her independence in 1810, and a few years afterward united with two other of Spain's revolted colonies in forming the old Colombian federal union, which was recognized by the United States in 1822. In 1836 this union was dissolved and Venezuela became again a separate and independent republic, being promptly recognized as such by our Government and by other powers.

Spain, however, halted in her recognition until 1845, when she quite superfluously ceded to Venezuela by treaty the territory which as an independent republic she had actually owned and possessed since 1810. But neither in this treaty nor in any other mention of the area of the republic were its boundaries described with more definiteness than as being "the same as those which marked the ancient viceroyalty and captaincy-general of New Granada and Venezuela in the year 1810."

England derived title to the colony of Guiana from Holland in 1814, by a treaty in which the territory was described as "the Cape of Good Hope and the establishments of Demerara, Essequibo, and Berbice." No boundaries of those settlements or "establishments" were given in the treaty, nor does it appear that any such boundaries had ever been particularly defined.

It is quite apparent that the limits of these adjoining countries thus lacking any mention of definite metes and bounds, were in need of extraneous assistance before they could be exactly fixed, and that their proper location was quite likely to lead to serious disagreement. In such circumstances threatening complications can frequently be avoided if the adjoining neighbors agree upon a divisional line promptly, and before their demands are stimulated and their tenacity increased by a real or fancied advance in the value of the possessions to be divided, or other incidents have intervened to render it more difficult to make concessions.

I shall not attempt to sketch the facts and arguments that bear upon the exact merits of this boundary controversy between Great Britain and Venezuela. They have been thoroughly examined by an arbitral tribunal to which the entire difficulty was referred, and by whose determination the boundary between the two countries has been fixed—perhaps in strict accord with justice, but at all events finally and irrevocably. Inasmuch, however, as our own country became in a sense involved in the controversy, or at least deeply concerned in its settlement, I have thought there might be interest in an explanation of the manner and the processes by which the interposition of the United States Government was brought about. I must not be expected to exclude from mention every circumstance that may relate to the merits of the dispute as between the parties primarily concerned; but so far as I make use of such circumstances I intend to do so only in aid and simplification of the explanation I have undertaken.

This dispute began in 1841. On October 5 of that year the Venezuelan minister to Great Britain, in a note to Lord Aberdeen, Principal Secretary of State for Foreign Affairs, after reminding the secretary that a proposal made by Venezuela on the 28th of January, 1841, for joint action in the matter of fixing a divisional boundary, still awaited the acceptance of Great Britain, wrote as follows:

> The Honorable Earl of Aberdeen may now judge of the surprise of the Government of Venezuela upon learning that in the territory of the Republic a sentry-box has been erected upon which the British flag has been raised. The Venezuelan Government is in ignorance of the origin and purport of these proceedings, and hopes that they may receive some satisfactory explanation of this action. In the meantime the undersigned, in compliance with the instructions communicated to him, urges upon the Honorable Earl of Aberdeen the necessity of entering into a treaty of boundaries as a previous step to the fixation of limits, and begs to ask for an answer to the above-mentioned communication of January 28.

Lord Aberdeen, in his reply, dated October 21, 1841, makes the following statement:

> Her Majesty's Government has received from the Governor of British Guiana, Mr. Schomburgk's report of his proceedings in execution of the commission with which he has been charged. That report states that Mr. Schomburgk set out from Demerara in April last and was on his return to the Essequibo River at the end of June. It appears that Mr. Schomburgk planted boundary posts at certain points of the country which he has surveyed, and that he was fully aware that the demarcation so made was merely a preliminary measure, open to further discussion between the Governments of Great Britain and Venezuela. But it does not appear that Mr. Schomburgk left behind him any guard-house, sentry-box, or other building having the British flag.

> With respect to the proposal of the Venezuelan Government that the Governments of Great Britain and Venezuela should conclude a treaty as a preliminary step to the demarcation of the boundaries between British Guiana and Venezuela, the undersigned begs leave to observe that it appears to him that if it should be necessary to make a treaty upon the subject of the boundaries in question, such a measure should follow rather than precede the operation of the survey.

In a communication dated the 18th of November, 1841, the Venezuelan minister, after again complaining of the acts of Schomburgk and alleging that he "has planted at a point on the mouth of the Orinoco several posts bearing Her Majesty's initials, and raised at the same place, with a show of armed forces, the British flag, and also performed several other acts of dominion and government," refers to the great dissatisfaction aroused in Venezuela by what he calls "this undeserved offense," and adds: "The undersigned therefore has no doubts but that he will obtain from Her Majesty's Government a reparation for the wrong done to the dignity of the Republic, and that those signs which have so unpleasantly shaken public confidence will be ordered removed."

No early response having been made to this communication, another was addressed to Lord Aberdeen, dated December 8, 1841, in which the representative of Venezuela refers to his previous unanswered note and to a recent order received from his government, which he says directs him "to insist not only upon the conclusion of a treaty fixing the boundaries between Venezuela and British Guiana, but also, and this very particularly, to insist upon the removal of the signs set up, contrary to all rights, by the surveyor R. H. Schomburgk in Barima and in other points of the Venezuelan territory"; and he continues: "In his afore-mentioned communication of the 18th of last month, the undersigned has already informed the Honorable Earl of Aberdeen of the dissatisfaction prevailing among the Venezuelans on this account, and now adds that this dissatisfaction, far from diminishing, grows stronger—as is but natural—as time goes on and no reparation of the wrongs is made."

These two notes of the Venezuelan minister were answered on the eleventh day of December, 1841. In his reply Lord Aberdeen says:

> The undersigned begs leave to refer to his note of the 21st of October last, in which he explained that the proceeding of Mr. Schomburgk in planting boundary posts at certain points of the country which he has surveyed was merely a preliminary measure open to future discussion between the two Governments, and that it would be premature to make a boundary treaty before the survey will be completed. The undersigned has only further to state that much unnecessary inconvenience would result from the removal of the posts fixed by Mr. Schomburgk, as they will afford the only tangible means by which Her Majesty's Government can be prepared to discuss the question of the boundaries with the Government of Venezuela. These posts were erected for that express purpose, and not, as the Venezuelan Government appears to apprehend, as

indications of dominion and empire on the part of Great Britain.

In a reply to this note, after referring to the explanation of the purpose of these posts or signs which Lord Aberdeen had given, it was said, in further urging their removal: "The undersigned regrets to be obliged to again insist upon this point; but the damages sustained by Venezuela on account of the permanence of said signs are so serious that he hopes in view of those facts that the trouble resulting from their removal may not appear useless." The minister followed this insistence with such earnest argument that on the thirty-first day of January, 1842, nearly four months after the matter was first agitated, Lord Aberdeen informed the Venezuelan minister that instructions would be sent to the governor of British Guiana directing him to remove the posts which had been placed by Mr. Schomburgk near the Orinoco. He, however, accompanied this assurance with the distinct declaration "that although, in order to put an end to the misapprehension which appears to prevail in Venezuela with regard to the object of Mr. Schomburgk's survey, the undersigned has consented to comply with the renewed representation of the Minister upon this affair, Her Majesty's Government must not be understood to abandon any portion of the rights of Great Britain over the territory which was formerly held by the Dutch in Guiana."

It should be here stated that the work which Schomburgk performed at the instance of the British Government consisted not only in placing monuments of some sort at the mouth of the Orinoco River, upon territory claimed by Venezuela, but also in locating from such monuments a complete dividing-line running far inland and annexing to British Guiana on the west a large region which Venezuela also claimed. This line, as originally located or as afterward still further extended to the west, came to be called "the Schomburgk line."

The Orinoco River, flowing eastward to the sea, is a very broad and deep waterway, which, with its affluents, would in any event, and however the bounds of Venezuela might be limited, traverse a very extensive portion of that country's area; and its control and free navigation are immensely important factors in the progress and prosperity of the republic. Substantially at the mouth of the Orinoco, and on its south side, two quite large rivers, the Barima and the Amacuro, flow into the sea. The region adjacent to the mouth of those rivers has, sometimes at least, been called Barima; and it was here that the posts or signs complained of by Venezuela were placed.

The coast from the mouth of the Orinoco River slopes or drops to the east and south; and some distance from that river's mouth, in the directions mentioned, the Essequibo, a large river flowing for a long distance from the south, empties into the sea.

After the correspondence I have mentioned, which resulted in the removal of the so-called initial monuments of the Schomburgk line from the Barima region, there seems to have been less activity in the boundary discussion until January 31, 1844, when the Venezuelan minister to England again addressed Lord Aberdeen on the subject. He referred to the erection of the Schomburgk monuments and the complaints of Venezuela on that account, and stated that since the removal of those monuments he had not ceased to urge Lord Aberdeen "to commence without delay negotiations for a treaty fixing definitely the boundary-line that shall divide the two countries." He adds the following very sensible statement: "Although it was undoubtedly the duty of the one who promoted this question to take the first step toward the negotiation of the treaty, the undersigned being well aware that other important matters claim the attention of Her Majesty's Government, and as he ought not to wait indefinitely, hastens to propose an agreement which, if left for a later date, may be difficult to conclude." It is disappointing to observe that the good sense exhibited in this statement did not hold out to the end of the minister's communication. After a labored presentation of historical incidents, beginning with the discovery of the American continent, he concludes by putting forward the Essequibo River as the proper boundary-line between the two countries. This was a proposition of such extreme pretensions that the Venezuelan representative knew, or ought to have known, it would not be considered for a moment by the Government of Great Britain; and it seems to me that a diplomatic error was made when, failing to apprehend the fact that the exigencies of the situation called for a show of concession, the Venezuelan minister, instead of intimating a disposition to negotiate, gave Great Britain an opportunity to be first in making proposals apparently calculated to meet the needs of conciliation and compromise.

Thus two months after the receipt of this communication,—on the thirtieth day of March, 1844,—Lord Aberdeen sent his reply. After combating the allegations contained in the letter of the Venezuelan representative, he remarked that if he were inclined to act upon the spirit of that letter, it was evident that he ought to claim on behalf of Great Britain, as the rightful successor to Holland, all the coast from the Orinoco to the Essequibo. Then follows this significant declaration:

> But the undersigned believes that the negotiations would not be free from difficulties if claims that cannot be sustained are presented, and shall not therefore follow Señor Fortique's example, but state here the concessions that Great Britain is disposed to make of her rights,

prompted by a friendly consideration for Venezuela and by her desire to avoid all cause of serious controversies between the two countries. Being convinced that the most important object for the interests of Venezuela is the exclusive possession of the Orinoco, Her Majesty's Government is ready to yield to the Republic of Venezuela a portion of the coast sufficient to insure her the free control of the mouth of this her principal river, and to prevent its being under the control of any foreign power.

Lord Aberdeen further declared that, "with this end in view, and being persuaded that a concession of the greatest importance has been made to Venezuela," he would consent on behalf of Great Britain to a boundary which he particularly defined, and in general terms may be described as beginning in the mouth of the Moroco River, which is on the coast southeast of the mouth of the Orinoco River and about two thirds of the distance between that point and the Essequibo River, said boundary running inland from that point until it included in its course considerably more territory than was embraced within the original Schomburgk line, though it excluded the region embraced within that line adjacent to the Barima and Amacuro rivers and the mouth of the Orinoco.

This boundary, as proposed by Lord Aberdeen, was not satisfactory to Venezuela; and soon after its submission her diplomatic representative died. This interruption was quickly followed by a long period of distressing internal strifes and revolutions, which so distracted and disturbed her government that for more than thirty years she was not in condition to renew negotiations for an adjustment of her territorial limits.

During all this time Great Britain seemed not especially unwilling to allow these negotiations to remain in abeyance.

This interval was not, however, entirely devoid of boundary incidents. In 1850 great excitement and indignation were aroused among the Venezuelans by a rumor that Great Britain intended to take possession of Venezuelan Guiana, a province adjoining British Guiana on the west, and a part of the territory claimed by Venezuela; and the feeling thus engendered became so extreme, both among the people and on the part of the government of the republic, that all remaining friendliness between the two countries was seriously menaced. Demonstrations indicating that Venezuela was determined to repel the rumored movement as an invasion of her rights, were met by instructions given by Great Britain to the commander of her Majesty's naval forces in the West Indies as to the course he was to pursue if the Venezuelan forces should construct fortifications within the territory in dispute. At the same time, Mr. Balford Hinton Wilson,

England's representative at Caracas, in a note addressed to the Minister of Foreign Affairs for Venezuela, indignantly characterized these disquieting rumors of Great Britain's intention to occupy the lands mentioned, as mischievous, and maliciously false; but he also declared that, on the other hand, her Majesty's Government would not see with indifference the aggressions of Venezuela upon the disputed territory.

This note contained, in addition, a rather impressive pronouncement in these words:

> The Venezuelan Government, in justice to Great Britain, cannot mistrust for a moment the sincerity of the formal declaration, which is now made in the name and by the express order of Her Majesty's Government, that Great Britain has no intention to occupy or encroach upon the territory in dispute; therefore the Venezuelan Government, in an equal spirit of good faith and friendship, cannot refuse to make a similar declaration to Her Majesty's Government, namely, that Venezuela herself has no intention to occupy or encroach upon the territory in dispute.

The Minister of Foreign Affairs for Venezuela responded to this communication in the following terms:

> The undersigned has been instructed by His Excellency the President of the Republic to give the following answer: The Government never could be persuaded that Great Britain, in contempt of the negotiation opened on the subject and the alleged rights in the question of limits pending between the two countries, would want to use force in order to occupy the land that each side claims— much less after Mr. Wilson's repeated assurance, which the Executive Power believes to have been most sincere, that those imputations had no foundation whatever, being, on the contrary, quite the reverse of the truth. Fully confident of this, and fortified by the protest embodied in the note referred to, the Government has no difficulty in declaring, as they do declare, that Venezuela has no intention of occupying or encroaching upon any portion of the territory the possession of which is in controversy; neither will she look with indifference on a contrary proceeding on the part of Great Britain.

In furtherance of these declarations the English Government stipulated that it would not "order or sanction such occupations or encroachments on the part of the British authorities"; and Venezuela agreed on her part to "instruct the authorities of Venezuelan Guiana to refrain from taking any step which might clash with the engagement hereby made by the Government."

I suspect there was some justification on each side for the accusations afterward interchanged between the parties that this understanding or agreement, in its strict letter and spirit, had not been scrupulously observed.

As we now pass from this incident to a date more than twenty-five years afterward, when attempts to negotiate for a settlement of the boundary controversy were resumed, it may be profitable, before going further, to glance at some of the conditions existing at the time of such resumption.

II

In 1876—thirty-two years after the discontinuance of efforts on the part of Great Britain and Venezuela to fix by agreement a line which should divide their possessions—Venezuela was confronted, upon the renewal of negotiations for that purpose, by the following conditions:

The claim by her, of a divisional line, founded upon her conception of strict right, which her powerful opponent had insisted could not in any way be plausibly supported, and which therefore she would in no event accept.

An indefiniteness in the limits claimed by Great Britain—so great that, of two boundary-lines indicated or suggested by her, one had been plainly declared to be "merely a preliminary measure open to future discussion between the Governments of Great Britain and Venezuela," while the other was distinctly claimed to be based not on any acknowledgment of the republic's rights, but simply upon generous concessions and a "desire to avoid all cause of serious controversies between the two countries."

A controversy growing out of this situation impossible of friendly settlement except by such arrangement and accommodation as would satisfy Great Britain, or by a submission of the dispute to arbitration.

A constant danger of such an extension of British settlements in the disputed territory as would necessarily complicate the situation and furnish a convenient pretext for the refusal of any concession respecting the lands containing such settlements.

A continual profession on the part of Great Britain of her present readiness to make benevolent concessions and of her willingness to co-operate in a speedy adjustment, while at the same time neither reducing her pretensions, nor attempting in a conspicuous manner to hasten negotiations to a conclusion.

A tremendous disparity in power and strength between Venezuela and her adversary, which gave her no hope of defending her territory or preventing its annexation to the possessions of Great Britain in case the extremity of force or war was reached.

The renewed negotiations began with a communication dated November 14, 1876, addressed by the Minister of Foreign Affairs for Venezuela to Lord Derby, then Great Britain's principal Secretary of State. In this communication the efforts made between the years 1841 and 1844 to establish by agreement a divisional line between the two countries, and their interruption, were referred to, and the earnest desire was expressed that negotiations for that purpose might at once be resumed. The minister suggested no other line than the Essequibo River, but in conclusion declared that the President of Venezuela was led to "hope that the solution of this question, already for so many years delayed, will be a work of very speedy and cordial agreement."

On the same day that this note was written to Lord Derby, one was also written by the same Venezuelan official to Mr. Fish, then our Secretary of State. After speaking of the United States as "the most powerful and the oldest of the Republics of the new continent, and called on to lend to others its powerful moral support in disputes with European nations," the minister directs attention to the boundary controversy between Venezuela and Great Britain and the great necessity of bringing it to a speedy termination. He concludes as follows: "But whatever may be the result of the new steps of the Government, it has desired that the American Government might at once take cognizance of them, convinced, as it is, that it will give the subject its kind consideration and take an interest in having due justice done to Venezuela." A memorandum was inclosed with the note, setting forth the claims of Venezuela touching the boundary location.

This appears to be the first communication addressed to our Government on the subject of a controversy in which we afterward became very seriously concerned.

A short time after the date of these communications, a Venezuelan envoy to Great Britain was appointed; and, on the thirteenth day of February, 1877, he addressed to Lord Derby a note in which, after asserting the right of Venezuela to insist upon the boundary previously claimed by her, he declared the willingness of his government "to settle this long-pending question in the most amicable manner," and suggested either the acceptance of a boundary-line such as would result from a presentation by both parties of Spanish and Dutch titles, maps, documents, and proofs existing before the advent in South America of either Venezuela or British Guiana, or the adoption of "a conventional line fixed by mutual accord between the Governments of Venezuela and Great Britain after a careful and friendly consideration of the case, keeping in view the documents presented by both sides, solely with the object of reconciling their mutual interests, and to fix a boundary as equitable as possible." The suggestion is made that the adoption of a divisional line is important "to prevent the occurrence of serious differences in the future, particularly as Guiana is attracting the general attention of the world on account of the immense riches which are daily being discovered there."

Let us here note that this renewal by Venezuela of her efforts to settle her boundary-line was accompanied by two new features. These, though in themselves entirely independent, became so related to each other, and in their subsequent combination and development they so imperiously affected our Government, that their coincident appearance at this particular stage of the controversy may well strike us as significant. One of these features was the abandonment by Venezuela of her insistence upon a line representing her extreme claims, and which England would not in any contingency accept, thus clearing the field for possible arbitration; and the other was her earnest appeal to us for our friendly aid. Neither should we fail to notice the new and important reference of the Venezuelan envoy to the immense riches being discovered in the disputed territory. Gold beneath soil in controversy does not always hasten the adjustment of uncertain or disputed boundary-lines.

On the twenty-fourth day of March, 1877, Lord Derby informed the Venezuelan envoy that the governor of British Guiana was shortly expected in London, and that he was anxious to await his arrival before taking any steps in the boundary discussion.

After waiting for more than two years for a further answer from the English Government, the Venezuelan representative in London, on the 19th of May, 1879, addressed a note on the subject to Lord Salisbury, who, in the meantime, had succeeded Lord Derby. In this note reference was made to the communication sent to Lord Derby in 1877, to the desire expressed by him to await the arrival of the governor of British Guiana before making reply, and to the fact that the communication mentioned still remained unanswered; and on behalf of Venezuela her representative repeated the alternative proposition made by him in February, 1877, in these words: "The boundary treaty may be based either on the acceptance of the line of strict right as shown by the records, documents, and other authoritative proofs which each party may exhibit, or on the acceptance at once by both Governments of a frontier of accommodation which shall satisfy the respective interests of the two countries"; and he concluded his note as follows:

> If Her Britannic Majesty's Government should prefer the frontier of accommodation or convenience, then it would be desirable that it should vouchsafe to make a proposition of an arrangement, on the understanding that, in order to obviate future difficulties and to give Great Britain the fullest proof of the consideration and friendship which Venezuela professes for her, my Government would not hesitate to accept a demarcation that should satisfy as far as possible the interests of the Republic.

> At all events, my Lord, something will have to be done to prevent this question from pending any longer.

> Thirty-eight years ago my Government wrote urging Her Majesty's Government to have the Boundary Treaty concluded, and now this affair is in the same position as in 1841, without any settlement; meanwhile Guiana has become of more importance than it was then, by reason of the large deposits of gold which have been and still are met with in that region.

Now, at the date of this communication England's most extreme claims were indicated either by the Schomburgk line or by the line which Lord Aberdeen suggested in 1844 as a concession. These were indeed the only lines which Great Britain had thus far presented. When in such circumstances, and with these lines distinctly in mind, the envoy of Venezuela offered to abandon for his country her most extreme claims, and asked that Great Britain should "vouchsafe to make a proposition of an arrangement" upon the basis of a "frontier of accommodation or convenience," what answer had he a right to expect? Most assuredly he had a right to expect that if Great Britain should prefer to proceed upon the theory of "accommodation or convenience," she would respond by offering such a reduction of the claims she had already made as would indicate a degree of concession or "accommodation" on her part that should entitle her to expect similar concession from Venezuela.

What was the answer actually made? After a delay of nearly eight months, on the tenth day of January, 1880, Lord Salisbury replied that her Majesty's Government were of the opinion that to argue the matter on the ground of strict right would involve so many intricate questions that it would be very unlikely to lead to a satisfactory solution of the question, and they would therefore prefer the alternative "of endeavoring to come to an agreement as to the acceptance by the two Governments of a frontier of accommodation which shall satisfy the respective interests of the two countries."

He then gives a most startling statement of the English Government's claim, by specifying boundaries which overlap the Schomburgk line and every other line that had been thought of or dreamed of before, declaring that such claim is justified "by virtue of ancient treaties with the aboriginal tribes and of subsequent cessions from Holland." He sets against this claim, or "on the other hand," as he says, the fact that the President of Venezuela, in a message dated February 20, 1877, "put forward a claim on the part of Venezuela to the river Essequibo as the boundary to which the Republic was entitled"—thereby giving prejudicial importance to a claim of boundary made by the President of Venezuela three years before, notwithstanding his Lordship was answering a communication in which Venezuela's present diplomatic representative distinctly proposed "a frontier of accommodation." His declaration, therefore, that the boundary which was thus put forward by the President of Venezuela would involve "the surrender of a province now inhabited by forty thousand British subjects," seems quite irrelevant, because such a boundary was not then under consideration; and in passing it may occur to us that the great delay in settling the boundaries between the two countries had given abundant opportunity for such inhabitation as Lord Salisbury suggests. His Lordship having thus built up a contention in which he puts on one side a line which for the sake of pacific accommodation Venezuela no longer proposes to insist upon, and on the other a line for Great Britain so grotesquely extreme as to appear fanciful, soberly observes:

> The difference, therefore, between these two claims is so great that it is clear that, in order to arrive at a satisfactory arrangement, each party must be prepared to make considerable concessions to the other; and although the claim of Venezuela to the Essequibo River boundary could not under any circumstances be entertained, I beg leave to assure you that Her Majesty's Government are anxious to meet the Venezuelan Government in a spirit of conciliation, and would be willing, in the event of a renewal of negotiations for a general settlement of boundaries, to waive a portion of what they consider to be their strict right, if Venezuela is really disposed to make corresponding concessions on her part.

And ignoring entirely the humbly respectful request of the Venezuelan minister that Great Britain would "vouchsafe to make a proposition of an arrangement," his Lordship thus concludes his communication: "Her

Majesty's Government will therefore be glad to receive, and will undertake to consider in the most friendly spirit, any proposal that the Venezuelan Government may think fit to make for the establishment of a boundary satisfactory to both nations."

This is diplomacy—of a certain sort. It is a deep and mysterious science; and we probably cannot do better than to confess our inability to understand its intricacies and sinuosities; but at this point we can hardly keep out of mind the methods of the shrewd, sharp trader who demands exorbitant terms, and at the same time invites negotiation, looking for a result abundantly profitable in the large range for dicker which he has created.

An answer was made to Lord Salisbury's note on the twelfth day of April, 1880, in which the Venezuelan envoy stated in direct terms that he had received specific instructions from his government for the arrangement of the difficulty, by abandoning the ground of strict right and "concurring in the adoption for both countries of a frontier mutually convenient, and reconciling in the best possible manner their respective interests—each party having to make concessions to the other for the purpose of attaining such an important result."

It will be remembered that in 1844, when this boundary question was under discussion, Lord Aberdeen proposed a line beginning in the mouth of the Moroco River, being a point on the coast south and east of the mouth of the Orinoco, thus giving to Venezuela the control of that river, but running inland in such a manner as to include, in the whole, little if any less area than that included in the Schomburgk line; and it will also be recalled that this line was not then acceptable to Venezuela. It appears, however, that the delays and incidents of thirty-six years had impressed upon the government of the republic the serious disadvantages of her situation in contention with Great Britain; for we find in this reply of the Venezuelan envoy the inquiry "whether Her Britannic Majesty's Government is disposed now, as it was in 1844, to accept the mouth of the river Moroco as the frontier at the coast." To this Lord Salisbury promptly responded that the attorney-general for the colony of British Guiana was shortly expected in England, and that her Majesty's Government would prefer to postpone the boundary discussion until his arrival.

This was followed by a silence of five months, with no word or sign from England's Foreign Office; and in the meantime Earl Granville had succeeded Lord Salisbury as Secretary of State for Foreign Affairs. After waiting thus long, the representative of Venezuela, on the 23d of September, 1880, reminded Lord Granville that in the preceding April his immediate predecessor had informed him that the arrival of the attorney-general of British Guiana was awaited before deciding the question of boundaries between the two Guianas; and as he had not, after the lapse of five months, been honored with a communication on the subject, he was bound to suppose that the attorney-general had not accomplished his voyage, in which case it was useless longer to wait for him. He further reminded his Lordship that on the 24th of March, 1877, Lord Derby, then in charge of British foreign affairs, also desired to postpone the consideration of the question until the arrival in London of the governor of British Guiana, who was then expected, but who apparently never came. He then proceeds as follows:

> Consequently it is best not to go on waiting either for the Governor or for the Attorney-General of the Colony, but to decide these questions ourselves, considering that my Government is now engaged in preparing the official map of the Republic and wishes of course to mark out the boundaries on the East.
>
> In my despatch of the 12th of April last, I informed your Excellency [Excellency's predecessor?] that as a basis of a friendly demarcation my Government was disposed to accept the mouth of the River Moroco as the frontier on the coast. If Her Britannic Majesty's Government should accept this point of departure, it would be very easy to determine the general course of the frontier, either by means of notes or in verbal conferences, as your Excellency might prefer.

On the twelfth day of February, 1881, Lord Granville, replying to Venezuela's two notes dated April 12 and September 23, 1880, informed her representative, without explanation, that her Majesty's Government would not accept the mouth of the Moroco as the divisional boundary on the coast.

A few days afterward, in an answer to this refusal, Venezuela's representative mentioned the extreme claims of the two countries and the fact that it had been agreed between the parties that steps should be taken to settle upon a frontier of accommodation; that in pursuance thereof he had proposed as the point of departure for such a frontier the mouth of the Moroco River, which was in agreement thus far with the proposition made by Lord Aberdeen on behalf of Great Britain in 1844; and pertinently added: "Thus thirty-seven years ago Her Britannic Majesty's Government spontaneously proposed the mouth of the Moroco River as the limit on the coast, a limit which your Excellency does not accept now, for you are pleased to tell me so in the note which I have the honor of answering." He thereupon suggests another boundary, beginning on the coast at a point one mile north of the mouth of the Moroco River and thence extending inland in such manner as to constitute a large concession on the part of Venezuela, but falling very far short of meeting the claims of Great Britain. He declares, however, that this demarcation "is the maximum of all concessions which in this matter the Government of Venezuela can grant by way of friendly arrangement."

Apparently anticipating, as he well might, that the boundary he proposed would fail of acceptance, he suggests that in such case the two governments would have no alternative but to determine the frontier by strict right, and that on this basis they would find it impossible to arrive at an agreement. Therefore he declares that he has received instructions from his government to urge upon Great Britain the submission of the question to an arbitrator, to be chosen by both parties, to whose award both governments should submit.

In this proposal of arbitration by Venezuela we find an approach to a new phase of the controversy. At first, the two countries had stood at arm's-length, each asserting strict right of boundary, only to be met by obstinate and unyielding resistance. Next, the field of mutual concession and accommodation had been traversed, with no result except damaging and dangerous delay. And now, after forty years of delusive hope, the time seemed at hand when the feebler contestant must contemplate ignominious submission to dictatorial exaction, or forcible resistance, futile and distressing, unless honorable rest and justice could be found in arbitration—the refuge which civilization has builded among the nations of the earth for the protection of the weak against the strong, and the citadel from which the ministries of peace issue their decrees against the havoc and barbarism of war.

The reply of Lord Granville to the communication of the envoy of Venezuela proposing an alternative of arbitration was delayed for seven months; and when, in September, 1881, it was received, it contained a rejection of the boundary offered by Venezuela and a proposal of a new line apparently lacking almost every feature of concession; and, singularly enough, there was not in this reply the slightest allusion to Venezuela's request for arbitration.

I do not find that this communication of Great Britain was ever specifically answered, though an answer was often requested. No further steps appear to have been taken until September 7, 1883, when Lord Granville instructed the British minister to Venezuela to invite the serious attention of the Venezuelan Government to the questions pending between the two countries, with a view to their early settlement. These questions are specified as relating to the boundary, to certain differential duties imposed on imports from British colonies, and to the claims of British creditors of the republic. His Lordship declared in those instructions that as a preliminary to entering upon negotiations it was indispensable that an answer should be given to the pending proposal which had been made by her Majesty's Government in regard to the boundary.

The representations made to the Government of Venezuela by the British minister, in obedience to those instructions, elicited a reply, in which a provision of the Venezuelan constitution was cited prohibiting the alienation or cession of any part of the territory of the republic; and it was suggested that, inasmuch as the Essequibo line seemed abundantly supported as the true boundary of Venezuela, a concession beyond that line by treaty would be obnoxious to this constitutional prohibition, whereas any reduction of territory brought about by a decree of an arbitral tribunal would obviate the difficulty. Therefore the urgent necessity was submitted for the selection of an arbitrator, "who, freely and unanimously chosen by the two Governments, would judge and pronounce a sentence of a definitive character."

The representative of her Majesty's Government, in a response dated February 29, 1884, commented upon the new difficulty introduced by the statement concerning the prohibition contained in the constitution of the republic, and expressed a fear that if arbitration was agreed to, the same prohibition might be invoked as an excuse for not abiding by an award unfavorable to Venezuela; and it was declared that if, on the other hand, the arbitrator should decide in favor of the Venezuelan Government to the full extent of their claim, "a large and important territory which has for a long period been inhabited and occupied by Her Majesty's subjects and treated as a part of the Colony of British Guiana would be severed from the Queen's dominions." This declaration is immediately followed by a conclusion in these words:

> For the above-mentioned reasons, therefore, the circumstances of the case do not appear to Her Majesty's Government to be such as to render arbitration applicable for a solution of the difficulty; and I have accordingly to request you, in making this known to the Venezuelan Government, to express to them the hope of Her Majesty's Government that some other means may be devised for bringing this long-standing matter to an issue satisfactory to both powers.

Let us pause here for a moment's examination of the surprising refusal of Great Britain to submit this difficulty to arbitration, and the more surprising reasons presented for its justification. The refusal was surprising because the controversy had reached such a stage that arbitration was evidently the only means by which it could be settled consistently with harmonious relations between the two countries.

It was on this ground that Venezuela proposed arbitration; and she strongly urged it on the further ground that inasmuch as the prohibition of her constitution prevented the relinquishment, by treaty or voluntary act, of any part of the territory which her people and their government claimed to be indubitably Venezuelan, such a relinquishment would present no difficulties if it was in obedience to a decree of a tribunal to which the question of ownership had been mutually submitted.

In giving her reasons for rejecting arbitration Great Britain says in effect: The plan you urge for the utter and complete elimination of this constitutional prohibition—for its expurgation and destruction so far as it is related to the pending dispute—is objectionable, because we fear the prohibition thus eliminated, expunged, and destroyed will still be used as a pretext for disobedience to an award which, for the express purpose of avoiding this constitutional restraint, you have invited.

The remaining objection interposed by Great Britain to the arbitration requested by Venezuela is based upon the fear that an award might be made in favor of the Venezuelan claim, in which case "a large and important territory which has for a long period been inhabited and occupied by Her Majesty's subjects and treated as a part of the Colony of British Guiana would be severed from the Queen's dominions."

It first occurs to us that a contention may well be suspected of weakness when its supporters are unwilling to subject it to the test of impartial arbitration. Certain inquiries are also pertinent in this connection. Who were the British subjects who had long occupied the territory that might through arbitration be severed from the Queen's dominions? How many of them began this occupancy during the more than forty years that the territory had been steadily and notoriously disputed? Did they enter upon this territory with knowledge of the dispute and against the warning of the government to which they owed allegiance, or were they encouraged and invited to such entry by agencies of that government who had full notice of the uncertainty of the British title? In one case, being themselves in the wrong, they were entitled to no consideration; in the other, the question of loss and indemnification should rest between them and their government, which had impliedly guaranteed them against disturbance. In any event, neither case presented a reason why Great Britain should take or possess the lands of Venezuela; nor did either case furnish an excuse for denying to Venezuela a fair and impartial adjudication of her disputed rights. By whom had this territory "been treated as a part of the Colony of British Guiana"? Surely not by Venezuela. On the contrary, she had persistently claimed it as her own, and had "treated" it as her own as far as she could and dared. England alone had treated it as a part of British Guiana; her immense power had enabled her to do this; and her decrees in her own favor as against her weak adversary undoubtedly promised greater advantages than arbitration could possibly assure.

III

The Secretary of State of Venezuela, soon after this refusal of Great Britain to submit the boundary dispute to arbitration, in a despatch dated the second day of April, 1884, still urged that method of settlement, citing precedents and presenting arguments in its favor; and in conclusion he asked the minister of the English Government at Caracas "to have the goodness to think out and suggest any acceptable course for attaining a solution of the difficulty." This was followed, a few days afterward, by another communication from the Venezuelan Secretary of State, repeating his urgent request for arbitration. From this communication it may not be amiss to make the following quotation:

> Venezuela and Great Britain possess the same rights in the question under discussion. If the Republic should yield up any part of her pretensions, she would recognize the superior right of Great Britain, would violate the above-quoted article of the Constitution, and draw down the censure of her fellow-citizens. But when both nations, putting aside their independence of action in deference to peace and good friendship, create by mutual consent a Tribunal which may decide in the controversy, the same is able to pass sentence that one of the two parties or both of them have been mistaken in their opinions concerning the extent of their territory. Thus the case would not be in opposition to the Constitution of the Republic, there being no alienation of that which shall have been determined not to be her property.

On the tenth day of June, 1884, arbitration was again refused in a curt note from Lord Granville, declaring that "Her Majesty's Government adhere to their objection to arbitration as a mode of dealing with this question."

About this time complaints and protests of the most vigorous character, based upon alleged breaches of the agreement of 1850 concerning the non-occupation of the disputed territory broke out on both sides of the controversy, and accusations of aggression and occupation were constantly made. I shall not attempt to follow them, as in detail they are not among the incidents which I consider especially relevant to the presentation of my theme.

On the thirteenth day of December, 1884, Venezuela, in reply to a proposition of the British Government that the boundary question and certain other differences should be settled simultaneously, suggested, in view of the unwillingness of Great Britain to submit the boundary dispute to arbitration, that it should be presented for decision to a court of law, the members of which should be chosen by the parties respectively.

The British Government promptly declined this proposition, and stated that they were not prepared to depart from the arrangement made in 1877 to decide the question by adopting a conventional boundary fixed by mutual accord between the two governments. This was in the face of the efforts which had been made along that line and found utterly fruitless.

Immediately following the last-mentioned proposition by Venezuela for the presentation of the difficulty to a court of law mutually chosen, negotiations were entered upon for the conclusion of a treaty between Great Britain and Venezuela, which should quiet a difference pending between the two countries relating to differential duties and which should also dispose of other unsettled questions. In a draft of such a treaty submitted by Venezuela there was inserted an article providing for arbitration in case of all differences which could not be adjusted by friendly negotiation. To this article Great Britain suggested an amendment, making such arbitration applicable only to matters arising out of the interpretation or execution of the treaty itself, and especially excluding those emanating from any other source; but on further representation by Venezuela, Lord Granville, in behalf of the Government of Great Britain, expressly agreed with Venezuela that the treaty article relating to arbitration should be unrestricted in its operation. This diplomatic agreement was in explicit terms, her Majesty's Government agreeing "that the undertaking to refer differences to arbitration shall include all differences which may arise between the High Contracting Parties, and not those only which arise on the interpretation of the Treaty."

This occurred on the fifteenth day of May, 1885. Whatever Lord Granville may have intended by the language used, the Government of Venezuela certainly understood his agreement to include the pending boundary dispute as among the questions that should be submitted to arbitration; and all other matters which the treaty should embrace seemed so easy of adjustment that its early completion, embodying a stipulation for the final arbitration of the boundary controversy, was confidently and gladly anticipated by the republic.

The high hopes and joyful anticipations of Venezuela born of this apparently favorable situation were, however, but short-lived.

On the twenty-seventh day of July, 1885, Lord Salisbury, who in the meantime had succeeded the Earl of Granville in Great Britain's Foreign Office, in a note to Venezuela's envoy, declared: "Her Majesty's Government are unable to concur in the assent given by their predecessors in office to the general arbitration article proposed by Venezuela, and they are unable to agree to the inclusion in it of matters other than those arising out of the interpretation or alleged violation of this particular treaty."

No assertion of the irrevocability of the agreement which Venezuela had made with his predecessor, and no plea or argument of any kind, availed to save the enlarged terms of this arbitration clause from Lord Salisbury's destructive insistence.

On the twentieth day of June, 1886, Lord Rosebery suggested for Great Britain, and as a solution of the difficulty, that the territory within two certain lines which had been already proposed as boundaries should be equally divided between the contestants, either by arbitration or the determination of a mixed commission.

This was declined by Venezuela on the twenty-ninth day of July, 1886, upon the same grounds that led to the declination of prior proposals that apparently involved an absolute cession of a part of her territory; and she still insisted upon an arbitration embracing the entire disputed territory as the only feasible method of adjustment.

This declination on the part of Venezuela of Lord Rosebery's proposition terminated the second attempt in point of time, to settle this vexed question. In the meantime the aggressive conduct which for some time the officials of both countries had exhibited in and near the contested region had grown in distinctness and significance, until Great Britain had openly and with notorious assertion of ownership taken possession of a valuable part of the territory in dispute. On the 26th of October, 1886, an official document was published in the London "Gazette" giving notice that no grants of land made by the Government of Venezuela in the territory claimed by Great Britain would be admitted or recognized by her Majesty; and this more significant statement was added: "A map showing the boundary between British Guiana and Venezuela claimed by Her Majesty's Government can be seen in the library of the Colonial Office, Downing Street, or at the Office of the Government Secretary, Georgetown, British Guiana." The boundary here spoken of, as shown on the map to which attention is directed, follows the Schomburgk line. Protests and demands in abundance on the part of Venezuela followed, which were utterly disregarded, until, on the thirty-first day of January, 1887, the Venezuelan Secretary of State distinctly demanded of Great Britain the evacuation of the disputed territory which she was occupying in violation of prior agreement and the rights of the republic, and gave formal notice that unless such evacuation should be completed, and accompanied by acceptance of arbitration as a means of deciding the pending frontier dispute, by the twentieth day of February, 1887, diplomatic relations between the two countries would on that day cease.

These demands were absolutely unheeded; and thereupon, when the twentieth day of February arrived, Venezuela exhibited a long list of specific charges of aggression and wrongdoing against Great Britain, and made the following statement and final protest:

> In consequence, Venezuela, not deeming it fitting to continue friendly relations with a state which thus injures her, suspends them from to-day.
>
> And she protests before the Government of Her Britannic Majesty, before all civilized nations, before the whole world, against the acts of spoliation which the Government of Great Britain has committed to her detriment, and which she will never on any consideration recognize as capable of altering in the slightest degree the rights which she has acquired from Spain, and respecting which she will be always ready to submit to a third power, as the only way to a solution compatible with her constitutional principles.

Notwithstanding all this, three years afterward, and on the tenth day of January, 1890, an agent of Venezuela, appointed for that purpose, addressed a note to Lord Salisbury, still in charge of Great Britain's foreign relations, expressing the desire of Venezuela to renew diplomatic relations with Great Britain, and requesting an interview to that end.

A short time thereafter the Government of Great Britain expressed its satisfaction that a renewal of diplomatic relations was in prospect, and presented to the representative of Venezuela "a statement of the conditions which Her Majesty's Government considered necessary for a satisfactory settlement of the questions pending between the two countries."

As the first of these conditions it was declared that "Her Majesty's Government could not accept as satisfactory any arrangement which did not admit the British title to the territory comprised within the line laid down by Sir R. Schomburgk in 1841; but they would be willing to refer to arbitration the claims of Great Britain to certain territory to the west of that line."

Naturally enough, this statement was received by Venezuela with great disappointment and surprise. Her representative promptly replied that his government could not accept any single point of the arbitrary and capricious line laid down by Sir R. Schomburgk in 1841, which had been declared null and void even by the Government of her Majesty; and that it was not possible for Venezuela to accept arbitration in respect to territory west of that line. He further expressed his regret that the conditions then demanded by Lord Salisbury were more unfavorable to Venezuela than the proposals made to the former agent of the republic prior to the suspension of diplomatic relations.

On the 19th of March, 1890, the British Government reiterated its position more in detail. Its refusal to admit any question as to Great Britain's title to any of the territory within the Schomburgk line was emphatically repeated, and the British claim was defined to extend beyond any pretension which I believe had ever been previously made except by Lord Salisbury himself in 1880. A map was presented indicating this extreme claim, the Schomburgk line, and a certain part of the territory between the boundary of this extreme claim on the west and the Schomburgk line, which Great Britain proposed to submit to arbitration, abandoning all claim to the remainder of the territory between these last-named two lines. This scheme, if adopted, would give to England absolutely and without question the large territory between British Guiana's conceded western boundary and the Schomburgk line, with an opportunity to lay claim before a board of arbitration for extensive additional territory beyond the Schomburgk line.

This is pitiful. The Schomburgk line, which was declared by the British Government, at the time it was made, to be "merely a preliminary measure, open to further discussion between the Governments of Great Britain and Venezuela," and which had been since largely extended in some mysterious way, is now declared to be a line so well established, so infallible, and so sacred that only the territory that England exorbitantly claims beyond that line is enough in dispute to be submitted to impartial arbitration. The trader is again in evidence. On this basis England could abundantly afford to lose entirely in the arbitration she at length conceded.

And yet Venezuela was not absolutely discouraged. Soon after the receipt of Great Britain's last depressing communication, she appointed still another agent who was to try his hand with England in the field of diplomacy. On the twenty-fourth day of June, 1890, this new representative replied to the above proposal made to his predecessor by her Majesty's

Government, and expressed the great regret of Venezuela that its recent proposals for a settlement of the boundary difficulty by arbitration affecting all the disputed territory had been peremptorily declined. He also declared that the emphatic statement contained in Great Britain's last communication in reference to this question created for his government "difficulties not formerly contemplated," and thereupon formally declined on behalf of Venezuela the consideration of the proposals contained in said communication. This statement of discouraging conditions was, however, supplemented by a somewhat new suggestion to the effect that a preliminary agreement should be made containing a declaration on the part of the Government of Venezuela that the river Essequibo, its banks, and the lands covering it belong exclusively to British Guiana, and a declaration on the part of her Majesty's Government that the Orinoco River, its banks, and the lands covering it belong exclusively to Venezuela, and providing that a mixed commission of two chief engineers and their staffs should be appointed to make, within one year, careful maps and charts of the region to the west and northwest of the Essequibo River, toward the Orinoco, in order to determine officially the exact course of its rivers and streams, and the precise position of its mountains and hills, and all other details that would permit both countries to have reliable official knowledge of the territory which was actually in dispute, enabling them to determine with a mutual feeling of friendship and good will a boundary with perfect knowledge of the case; but in the event that a determination should not be thus reached, the final decision of the boundary question should be submitted to two arbitrators, one selected by each government, and a third chosen by the other two, to act as umpire in case of disagreement, who, in view of the original titles and documents presented, should fix a boundary-line which, being in accordance with the respective rights and titles, should have the advantage as far as possible of constituting a natural boundary; and that, pending such determination, both governments should remove or withdraw all posts and other indications and signs of possession or dominion on said territory, and refrain from exercising any jurisdiction within the disputed region.

On the 24th of July, 1890, Lord Salisbury declined to accept these suggestions of the Venezuelan representative, and declared: "Her Majesty's Government have more than once explained that they cannot consent to submit to arbitration what they regard as their indisputable title to districts in the possession of the British Colony."

Is it uncharitable to see in this reference to "possession" a hint of the industrious manner in which Great Britain had attempted to improve her position by permitting colonization, and by other acts of possession, during the half-century since the boundary dispute began?

Efforts to settle this controversy seem to have languished after this rebuff until March, 1893, when still another agent was appointed by Venezuela for the purpose of reëstablishing diplomatic relations with Great Britain, and settling, if possible, the boundary trouble and such other differences as might be pending between the two countries. As a means to that end, this agent, on the twenty-sixth day of May, 1893, presented a memorandum to the British Government containing suggestions for such settlement. The suggestion relating to the adjustment of the boundary question rested upon the idea of arbitration and did not materially differ from that made by this agent's immediate predecessor in 1890, except as to the *status quo*, pending final adjustment, which it was proposed should be the same as that existing after the agreement of non-interference in the disputed territory made by the two governments in 1850.

The plan thus suggested was declined by the Government of Great Britain, because, in the first place, it involved an arbitration, "which had been repeatedly declined by Her Majesty's Government," and, further, because it was, in the language of the British reply, "quite impossible that they should consent to revert to the *status quo* of 1850 and evacuate what has for some years constituted an integral portion of British Guiana."

A further communication from the agent of Venezuela, offering additional arguments in support of his suggestions, brought forth a reply informing him that the contents of his note did not "appear to Her Majesty's Government to afford any opening for arriving at an understanding on this question which they could accept."

Six months afterward, on the twenty-ninth day of September, 1893, a final communication was addressed by the representative of Venezuela to the British Government, reviewing the situation and the course of past efforts to arrive at a settlement, and concluding with the words:

> I must now declare in the most solemn manner, and in the name of the Government of Venezuela, that it is with the greatest regret that that Government sees itself forced to leave the situation produced in the disputed territory by the acts of recent years unsettled, and subject to the serious disturbances which acts of force cannot but produce; and to declare that Venezuela will never consent to proceedings of that nature being accepted as title-deeds to justify the arbitrary occupation of territory which is within its jurisdiction.

Here closed a period in this dispute, fifty-two years in duration, vexed with agitation, and perturbed by irritating and repeated failures to reach a peaceful adjustment. Instead of progress in the direction of a settlement of their boundaries, the results of their action were increased obstacles to fair discussion, intensified feelings of injury, extended assertion of title, ruthless appropriation of the territory in controversy, and an unhealed breach in diplomatic relations.

IV

I have thus far dealt with this dispute as one in which Great Britain and Venezuela, the parties primarily concerned, were sole participants. We have now, however, reached a stage in the affair which requires a recital of other facts which led up to the active and positive interference of our own Government in the controversy. In discussing this branch of our topic it will be necessary not only to deal with circumstances following those already narrated, but to retrace our steps sufficiently to exhibit among other things the appeals and representations made to the Government of the United States by Venezuela, while she was still attempting to arrive at an adjustment with Great Britain.

I have already referred to the first communication made to us by Venezuela on the subject. This, it will be remembered, was in 1876, when she sought to resume negotiations with Great Britain, after an interruption of thirty-two years. I have also called attention to the fact that coincident with this communication Venezuela presented to Great Britain a willingness to relax her insistence upon her extreme boundary claim, based upon alleged right, and suggested that a conventional line might be fixed by mutual concession.

Venezuela's first appeal to us for support and aid amounted to little more than a vague and indefinite request for countenance and sympathy in her efforts to settle her differences with her contestant, with an expression of a desire that we would take cognizance of her new steps in that direction. I do not find that any reply was made to this communication.

Five years afterward, in 1881, the Venezuelan minister in Washington presented to Mr. Evarts, then our Secretary of State, information he had received that British vessels had made their appearance in the mouth of the Orinoco River with materials to build a telegraph-line, and had begun to erect poles for that purpose at Barima: and he referred to the immense importance to his country of the Orinoco; to the efforts of his government to adjust her difficulty with Great Britain, and to the delays interposed; and finally expressed his confident belief that the United States would not view with indifference what was being done in a matter of such capital importance.

Mr. Evarts promptly replied, and informed the Venezuelan representative that "in view of the deep interest which the Government of the United States takes in all transactions tending to attempted encroachments of foreign powers upon the territory of any of the republics of this continent, this Government could not look with indifference to the forcible acquisition of such territory by England, if the mission of the vessels now at the mouth of the Orinoco should be found to be for that end."

Again, on the thirtieth day of November, 1881, our minister to Venezuela reported to Mr. Blaine, who had succeeded Mr. Evarts as Secretary of State, an interview with the President of Venezuela at his request, in which the subject of the boundary dispute was discussed. Our minister represented that the question was spoken of by the President as being of essential importance and a source of great anxiety to him, involving a large and fertile territory between the Essequibo and Orinoco, and probably the control of the mouth and a considerable portion of the latter river; and he alleged that the policy of Great Britain, in the treatment of this question, had been delay—the interval being utilized by gradually but steadily extending her interest and authority into the disputed territory; and "that, though the rights of Venezuela were clear and indisputable, he questioned her ability, unaided by some friendly nation, to maintain them."

In July, 1882, Mr. Frelinghuysen, successor to Mr. Blaine, sent to our representative at Venezuela a despatch to be communicated to the government of the republic, in which he stated that, if Venezuela desired it, the United States would propose to the Government of Great Britain that the boundary question be submitted to the arbitrament of a third power.

It will be remembered that a proposition for arbitration had been made by Venezuela to Great Britain in February, 1881, and that Great Britain had refused to accede to it.

In July, 1884, Mr. Frelinghuysen sent a confidential despatch to Mr. Lowell, our minister to Great Britain, informing him that Guzman Blanco, ex-President of Venezuela, who had recently been accredited as a special envoy from his country to Great Britain, had called on him relative to the objects of his mission, in respect of which he desired to obtain the good offices of this Government, and that doubtless he would seek to confer with Mr. Lowell in London. He further informed Mr. Lowell that he had told the Venezuelan envoy that, "in view of our interest in all that touches the independent life of the Republics of the American Continent, the United States could not be indifferent to anything that might impair their normal self-control"; that "the moral position of the United States in these matters was well known through the enunciation of the Monroe Doctrine," though formal action in the direction of applying that doctrine to a speculative case affecting Venezuela seemed to him to be inopportune, and therefore he could not advise Venezuela to arouse a discussion of that point. He instructed our minister to show proper consideration to the Venezuelan envoy, and to "take proper occasion to let Lord Granville know that we are not without concern as to whatever may affect the interest of a sister Republic of the American Continent and its position in the family of nations."

In July, 1885, the Venezuelan minister to the United States addressed a communication to Secretary of State Bayard, setting forth the correspondence which had already taken place between our Government and that of Venezuela touching the boundary dispute, and referring to the serious condition existing on account of the renewed aggressions of Great Britain.

Mr. Bayard thereupon sent a despatch on the subject to Mr. Phelps, our diplomatic representative to England, in which, after stating that the Venezuelan Government had never definitely declared what course she desired us to pursue, but, on the contrary, had expressed a desire to be guided by our counsel, he said: "The good offices of this Government have been tendered to Venezuela to suggest to Great Britain the submission of the boundary dispute to arbitration; but when shown that such action on our part would exclude us from acting as arbitrator, Venezuela ceased to press the matter in that direction"; and the next day after writing this despatch Mr. Bayard informed the Venezuelan minister that the President of the United States could not entertain a request to act as umpire in any dispute unless it should come concurrently from both contestants.

In December, 1886, our minister to Venezuela addressed a despatch to Mr. Bayard, in which he reported that matters looked very angry and threatening in Venezuela on account of fresh aggressions on the part of Great Britain in the disputed territory; and he expressed the fear that an open rupture might occur between the two countries. He inclosed a statement made by the Venezuelan Minister of Foreign Affairs, containing a list of grievances, followed by this declaration: "Venezuela, listening to the advice of the United States, has endeavored several times to obtain that the difference should be submitted to the award of a third power.... But such efforts have proven fruitless, and the possibility of that result, the only one prescribed by our constitution, being arrived at, becomes more and more remote from day to day. Great Britain has been constant in her clandestine advances upon the Venezuelan territory, not taking into consideration either the rights or the complaints of this Republic." And he adds the following declaration: "Under such circumstances the Government has but two courses left open: either to employ force in order to recover places from which force has ejected the Republic, since its amicable representations on the subject have failed to secure redress, or to present a solemn protest to the Government of the United States against so great an abuse, which is an evident declaration of war—a provocative aggression."

Thereupon, and on the twentieth day of December, 1886, a despatch was sent by Mr. Bayard to Mr. Phelps, in which the secretary comments on the fact that at no time theretofore had the good offices of our Government been actually tendered to avert a rupture between Great Britain and Venezuela, and that our inaction in this regard seemed to be due to the reluctance of Venezuela to have the Government of the United States take any steps having relation to the action of the British Government which might, in appearance even, prejudice the resort to our arbitration or mediation which Venezuela desired; but that the intelligence now received warranted him in tendering the good offices of the United States to promote an amicable settlement of the difficulty between the two countries, and offering our arbitration if acceptable to both countries—as he supposed the dispute turned upon simple and readily ascertainable historical facts.

Additional complaints against Great Britain on account of further trespasses on Venezuelan territory were contained in a note from the Venezuelan minister to Mr. Bayard, dated January 4, 1887. I shall quote only the following passage:

> My Government has tried all possible means to induce that of London to accept arbitration, as advised by the United States; this, however, has resulted in nothing but fresh attempts against the integrity of the territory by the colonial authorities of Demerara. It remains to be seen how long my Government will find it possible to exercise forbearance transcending the limits of its positive official duty.

Pursuant to his instructions from Mr. Bayard, our minister to Great Britain formally tendered to the English Government, on the eighth day of February, 1887, the good offices of the United States to promote an amicable settlement of the pending controversy, and offered our arbitration, if acceptable to both parties.

A few days afterward Lord Salisbury, on behalf of Great Britain, replied that the attitude which had been taken by the President of the Venezuelan republic precluded her Majesty's Government from submitting the question at that time to the arbitration of any third power.

The fact that Lord Salisbury had declined our offer of mediation and arbitration, was promptly conveyed to the government of Venezuela; and thereupon, on the fourth day of May, 1887, her minister at Washington addressed another note to our Secretary of State indicating much depression on account of the failure of all efforts up to that time made to induce Great Britain to agree to a settlement of the controversy by arbitration, and expressing the utmost gratitude for the steps taken by our Government in aid of those efforts. He also referred to the desire his government once entertained that, in case arbitration could be attained, the United States might be selected as arbitrator, and to the fact that this desire had been relinquished because the maintenance of impartiality essential in an arbitrator would "seriously impair the efficiency of action which for the furtherance of the common interests of America, and in obedience to the doctrine of the immortal Monroe, should possess all the vitality that the alarming circumstances demand"; and he begged the secretary to instruct our representative in London "to insist, in the name of the United States Government, upon the necessity of submitting the boundary question between Venezuela and British Guiana to arbitration."

I have heretofore refrained from stating in detail the quite numerous instances of quarrel and collision that occurred in and near the disputed territory, with increasing frequency, during this controversy. One of these, however, I think should be here mentioned. It seems that in 1883 two vessels belonging to English subjects were seized and their crews taken into custody by Venezuelan officials in the disputed region, for alleged violations of the laws of Venezuela within her jurisdiction, and that English officials had assumed, without any judicial determination and without any notice to Venezuela, to assess damages against her on account of such seizure and arrests, in an amount which, with interest, amounted in 1887 to about forty thousand dollars. On the seventh day of October in that year, the governor of Trinidad, an English island near the mouth of the Orinoco, in a letter to the Minister of Foreign Affairs for Venezuela, declared that her Majesty's Government could not permit such injuries to remain unredressed, or their representations to be disregarded any longer, and thereupon it was demanded that the money claimed, with interest, be paid within seven days from the delivery of said letter. The letter concluded as follows:

Failing compliance with the above demands Her Majesty's Government will be reluctantly compelled to instruct the Commander of Her Majesty's naval forces in the West Indies to take such measures as he may deem necessary to obtain that reparation which has been vainly sought for by friendly means; and in case of so doing they will hold the

Venezuelan Government responsible for any consequences that may arise.

Venezuela did not fail to appreciate and frankly acknowledge that, in her defenseless condition, there was no escape from the payment of the sum which England, as a judge in its own cause, had decreed against her. The President of the republic, however, in a prompt reply to the governor's note, characterized its terms as "offensive to the dignity of the nation and to the equality which, according to the principles of the rights of nations, all countries enjoy without any regard to their strength or weakness." Thereupon he sought the good offices of our minister to Venezuela in an effort to procure a withdrawal of the objectionable communication. This was attempted in a note sent by the American minister to the governor of Trinidad, in which he said:

> I hope your Excellency will permit me to suggest, as a mutual friend of both parties, the suspension or withdrawal of your note of the 7th instant, so that negotiations may at once be opened for the immediate and final settlement of the afore-mentioned claims without further resort to unpleasant measures. From representations made to me, I am satisfied that if the note of the 7th instant is withdrawn temporarily even, Venezuela will do in the premises that which will prove satisfactory to your Government.

A few days after this note was sent, a reply was received in which the governor of Trinidad courteously expressed his thanks to our minister for his good offices, and informed him that, as the Government of Venezuela regarded his note of October 7 "as offensive, and appeared desirous of at last settling this long-pending question in a friendly spirit," he promptly telegraphed to her Majesty's Government asking permission to withdraw that note and substitute a less forcible one for it; and that he had just been informed by his home government in reply that this arrangement could not be sanctioned.

Our minister reported this transaction to his home government at Washington on the fourth day of November, 1887, and stated that the money demanded by Great Britain had been paid by Venezuela under protest.

Venezuela may have been altogether at fault in the transaction out of which this demand arose; the amount which England exacted may not have been unreasonable; and the method of its assessment, though not the most considerate possible, has support in precedent; and even the threat of a naval force may sometimes be justified in enforcing unheeded demands. I have not adverted to this incident for the purpose of inviting judgment on any of its phases, but only to call attention to the fact that it was allowed to culminate with seemingly studied accompaniments of ruthlessness and irritation, at a time when a boundary question was pending between the two nations, when the weaker contestant was importuning the stronger for arbitration, and when a desire for reconciliation and peace in presence of strained relations should have counseled considerateness and magnanimity—all this in haughty disregard of the solicitous and expressed desire of the Government of the United States to induce a peaceful adjustment of the boundary dispute, and in curt denial of our request that this especially disturbing incident should be relieved of its most exasperating features.

In the trial of causes before our courts, evidence is frequently introduced to show the animus or intent of litigating parties.

Perhaps strict decorum hardly permits us to adopt the following language, used by the Venezuelan minister when reporting to our Secretary of State the anticipated arrival of a British war-steamer to enforce the demand of Great Britain:

> Such alarming news shows evidently that the Government of Her Britannic Majesty, encouraged by the impunity on which it has counted until now for the realization of its unjust designs with regard to Venezuela, far from procuring a pacific and satisfactory agreement on the different questions pending with the latter, is especially eager to complicate in order to render less possible every day that equitable solution which has been so fully the endeavor of my people.

On the fifteenth day of February, 1888, the Venezuelan minister, in communicating to our Government information he had received touching a decree of the governor of Demerara denying the validity of a contract entered into by the Government of Venezuela for the construction of a railway between certain points in the territory claimed by Venezuela, commented on the affair as follows:

> England has at last declared emphatically that her rights are without limit, and embrace whatever regions may be suggested to her by her insatiate thirst for conquest. She even goes so far as to deny the validity of railway grants comprised within territory where not even the wildest

dream of fancy had ever conceived that the day would come when Venezuela's right thereto could be disputed. The fact is that until now England has relied upon impunity. She beholds in us a weak and unfriended nation, and seeks to make the Venezuelan coast and territories the base of a conquest which, if circumstances are not altered, will have no other bounds than the dictates of her own will.

V

Mr. Bayard, in a despatch transmitting this to our minister to England, says that our Government has heretofore acted upon the assumption that the boundary controversy between Great Britain and Venezuela was one based on historical facts, which without difficulty could be determined according to evidence, but that the British pretension now stated gives rise to grave disquietude, and creates the apprehension that their territorial claim does not follow historical traditions or evidence, but is apparently indefinite. He refers to the British Colonial Office list of previous years, and calls attention to the wide detour to the westward in the boundaries of British Guiana between the years 1877 and 1887, as shown in that record. He suggests that our minister "express anew to Lord Salisbury the great gratification it would afford our Government to see the Venezuelan dispute amicably and honorably settled by arbitration or otherwise," and adds: "If indeed it should appear that there is no fixed limit to the British boundary claim, our good disposition to aid in a settlement might not only be defeated, but be obliged to give place to a feeling of grave concern."

It was about this time that the Venezuelan minister, in a note expressing his appreciation of our efforts to bring about a settlement of the dispute, made the following statement:

> Disastrous and fatal consequences would ensue for the independence of South America if, under the pretext of a question of boundaries, Great Britain should succeed in consummating the usurpation of a third part of our territory, and therewith a river so important as the Orinoco. Under the pretext of a mere question of boundaries which began on the banks of the Essequibo, we now find ourselves on the verge of losing regions lying more than five degrees away from that river.

On May 1, 1890, Mr. Blaine, Mr. Bayard's successor as Secretary of State, instructed Mr. Robert T. Lincoln, our minister to England, "to use his good offices with Lord Salisbury to bring about the resumption of diplomatic intercourse between Great Britain and Venezuela as a preliminary step toward the settlement of the boundary dispute by arbitration." He also requested him "to propose to Lord Salisbury, with a view to an accommodation, that an informal conference be had in Washington or in London of representatives of the three powers." The secretary added: "In such conference the position of the United States is one solely of impartial friendship toward both litigants."

In response to this instruction Mr. Lincoln had an interview with Lord Salisbury. On this occasion his Lordship said that her Majesty's Government had not for some time been keen in attempts to settle the dispute, in view of their feeling of uncertainty as to the stability of the present Venezuelan Government and the frequency of revolutions in that quarter; but that he would take pleasure in considering our suggestion after consulting the Colonial Office, to which it would first have to be referred. Mr. Lincoln, in giving his impressions derived from the interview, says that "while Lord Salisbury did not intimate what would probably be the nature of his reply, there was certainly nothing unfavorable in his manner of receiving the suggestion"; and he follows this with these significant words: "If the matter had been entirely new and dissociated with its previous history, I should have felt from his tone that the idea of arbitration in some form, to put an end to the boundary dispute, was quite agreeable to him."

On the 26th of May, 1890, Lord Salisbury addressed a note to Mr. Lincoln, in which his Lordship stated that her Majesty's Government was at that moment in communication with the Venezuelan minister in Paris, who had been authorized to express the desire of his Government for the renewal of diplomatic relations, and to discuss the conditions on which it might be effected; that the terms on which her Majesty's Government considered that a settlement of the question in issue between the two countries might be made, had been communicated to Venezuela's representative; that his reply was still awaited, and that the British Government "would wish to have the opportunity of examining that reply, and ascertaining what prospect it would afford of an adjustment of existing differences, before considering the expediency of having recourse to the good offices of a third party."

No mention was made, in this communication, nor at any time thereafter, so far as I can discover, of Mr. Blaine's proposal of a conference among representatives of the three nations interested in an adjustment.

Lord Salisbury, in a despatch to the English representative at Washington, dated November 11, 1891, stated that our minister to England had, in conversation with him, renewed, on the part of our Government, the expression of a hope that the Government of Great Britain would refer the boundary dispute to arbitration; that his Lordship had expressed his willingness to submit to arbitration all the questions which seemed to his government to be fairly capable of being treated as questions of controversy; that the principal obstacle was the rupture of diplomatic relations caused by Venezuela's act; and that before the Government of Great Britain could renew negotiations they must be satisfied that those relations were about to be resumed with a prospect of their continuance.

While our Government was endeavoring to influence Great Britain in the direction of fair and just arbitration, and receiving for our pains only barren assurances and procrastinating excuses, the appeals of Venezuela for help, stimulated by allegations of constantly increasing English pretensions, were incessantly ringing in our ears.

Without mentioning a number of these appeals, and passing over a period of more than two years, I shall next refer to a representation made by the Venezuelan minister at Washington on March 31, 1894, to Mr. Gresham, who was then our Secretary of State. In this communication the course of the controversy and the alleged unauthorized acts of England from the beginning to that date were rehearsed with circumstantial particularity. The conduct of Great Britain in refusing arbitration was again reprobated, and pointed reference was made to a principle which had been asserted by the United States, "that the nations of the American continent, after having acquired the liberty and independence which they enjoy and maintain, were not subject to colonization by any European power." The minister further declared that "Venezuela has been ready to adhere to the conciliatory counsel of the United States that a conference, consisting of its own Representative and those of the two parties, should meet at Washington or London for the purpose of preparing an honorable reëstablishment of harmony between the litigants," and that "Great Britain has disregarded the equitable proposition of the United States."

On July 13, 1894, Mr. Gresham sent a despatch to Mr. Bayard, formerly Secretary of State, but then ambassador to England, inclosing the communication of the Venezuelan minister, calling particular attention to its contents, and at the same time briefly discussing the boundary dispute. In this despatch Mr. Gresham said:

> The recourse to arbitration first proposed in 1881, having been supported by your predecessors, was in turn advocated by you, in a spirit of friendly regard for the two

nations involved. In the meantime successive advances of British settlers in the region admittedly in dispute were followed by similar advances of British Colonial administration, contesting and supplanting Venezuelan claims to exercise authority therein.

He adds: "Toward the end of 1887, the British territorial claim, which had, as it would seem, been silently increased by some twenty-three thousand square miles between 1885 and 1886, took another comprehensive sweep westward to embrace" a certain rich mining district. "Since then," the secretary further states, "repeated efforts have been made by Venezuela as a directly interested party, and by the United States as the impartial friend of both countries, to bring about a resumption of diplomatic relations, which had been suspended in consequence of the dispute now under consideration."

This despatch concludes as follows:

The President is inspired by a desire for a peaceable and honorable adjustment of the existing difficulties between an American state and a powerful transatlantic nation, and would be glad to see the reëstablishment of such diplomatic relations between them as would promote that end. I can discover but two equitable solutions to the present controversy. One is the arbitral determination of the rights of the disputants as the respective successors to the historical rights of Holland and Spain over the region in question. The other is to create a new boundary-line in accordance with the dictates of mutual expediency and consideration. The two Governments having so far been unable to agree on a conventional line, the consistent and conspicuous advocacy by the United States and England of the principle of arbitration, and their recourse thereto in settlement of important questions arising between them, makes such a mode of adjustment especially appropriate in the present instance; and this Government will gladly do what it can to further a determination in that sense.

In another despatch to Mr. Bayard, dated December 1, 1894, Mr. Gresham says:

I cannot believe Her Majesty's Government will maintain that the validity of their claim to territory long in dispute between the two countries shall be conceded as a condition precedent to the arbitration of the question whether Venezuela is entitled to other territory, which until a recent period was never in doubt. Our interest in the question has repeatedly been shown by our friendly efforts to further a settlement alike honorable to both countries, and the President is pleased to know that Venezuela will soon renew her efforts to bring about such an adjustment.

Two days afterward, on December 3, 1894, the President's annual message was sent to the Congress, containing the following reference to the controversy:

> The boundary of British Guiana still remains in dispute between Great Britain and Venezuela. Believing that its early settlement on some just basis alike honorable to both parties is in the line of our established policy to remove from this hemisphere all causes of difference with powers beyond the sea, I shall renew the efforts heretofore made to bring about a restoration of diplomatic relations between the disputants and to induce a reference to arbitration—a resort which Great Britain so conspicuously favors in principle and respects in practice, and which is earnestly sought by her weaker adversary.

On the twenty-second day of February, 1895, a joint resolution was passed by the Congress, earnestly recommending to both parties in interest the President's suggestion "that Great Britain and Venezuela refer their dispute as to boundaries to friendly arbitration."

A despatch dated February 23, 1895, from Great Britain's Foreign Office to the English ambassador at Washington, stated that on the twenty-fifth day of January, 1895, our ambassador, Mr. Bayard, had, in an official interview, referred to the boundary controversy, and said "that his Government would gladly lend their good offices to bring about a settlement by means of an arbitration." The despatch further stated that Mr. Bayard had thereupon been informed that her Majesty's Government had expressed their willingness to submit the question, within certain limits, to arbitration, but could not agree to the more extensive reference on which the Venezuelan Government insisted; that Mr. Bayard called again on the twentieth day of February, when a memorandum was read to him concerning the situation and a map shown him of the territory in dispute; that at the same time he was informed that the Venezuelans had recently made an aggression upon the territory of English occupation, and, according to report, ill-treated some of the colonial police stationed there, and that it was the boundary defined by the Schomburgk line which had thus been violated in a marked manner by the Venezuelans.

This despatch concludes as follows:

> On Mr. Bayard's observing that the United States Government was anxious to do anything in their power to facilitate a settlement of the difficulty by arbitration, I reminded his Excellency that although Her Majesty's Government were ready to go to arbitration as to a certain portion of the territory which I had pointed out to him, they could not consent to any departure from the Schomburgk line.

It now became plainly apparent that a new stage had been reached in the progress of our intervention, and that the ominous happenings embraced within a few months had hastened the day when we were challenged to take our exact bearings, lest we should miss the course of honor and national duty. The more direct tone that had been given to our despatches concerning the dispute, our more insistent and emphatic suggestion of arbitration, the serious reference to the subject in the President's message, the significant resolution passed by Congress earnestly recommending arbitration, all portended a growth of conviction on the part of our Government concerning this controversy, which gave birth to pronounced disappointment and anxiety when Great Britain, concurrently with these apprising incidents, repeated in direct and positive terms her refusal to submit to arbitration except on condition that a portion of the disputed territory which Venezuela had always claimed to be hers should at the outset be irrevocably conceded to England.

During a period of more than fourteen years our Government, assuming the character of a mutual and disinterested friend of both countries, had, with varying assiduity, tendered its good offices to bring about a pacific and amicable settlement of this boundary controversy, only to be repelled with more or less civility by Great Britain. We had seen her pretensions in the disputed regions widen and extend in such manner and upon such pretexts as seemed to constitute an actual or threatened violation of a doctrine which our nation long ago established, declaring that the American continents are not to be considered subjects for future colonization by any European power; and despite all this we had, nevertheless, hoped, during all these years, that arrangement and accommodation between the principal parties would justify us in keeping an invocation of that doctrine in the background of the discussion. Notwithstanding, however, all our efforts to avoid it, we could not be unmindful of the conditions which the progress of events had created, and whose meaning and whose exigencies inexorably confronted us. England had finally and unmistakably declared that all the territory embraced within the Schomburgk line was indisputably hers. Venezuela presented a claim to territory within the same limits, which could not be said to lack strong support. England had absolutely refused to permit Venezuela's claim to be tested by arbitration; and Venezuela was utterly powerless to resist by force England's self-pronounced decree of ownership. If this decree was not justified by the facts, and it should be enforced against the protest and insistence of Venezuela and should result in the possession and colonization of Venezuelan territory by Great Britain, it seemed quite plain that the American doctrine which denies to European powers the colonization of any part of the American continent would be violated.

If the ultimatum of Great Britain as to her claim of territory had appeared to us so thoroughly supported upon the facts as to admit of small doubt, we might have escaped the responsibility of insisting on an observance of the Monroe Doctrine in the premises, on our own account, and have still remained the disinterested friend of both countries, merely contenting ourselves with benevolent attempts to reconcile the disputants. We were, however, far from discovering such satisfactory support in the evidence within our reach. On the contrary, we believed that the effects of our acquiescence in Great Britain's pretensions would amount to a failure to uphold and maintain a principle universally accepted by our Government and our people as vitally essential to our national integrity and welfare. The arbitration, for which Venezuela pleaded, would have adjudged the exact condition of the rival claims, would have forever silenced Venezuela's complaints, and would have displaced by conclusive sentence our unwelcome doubts and suspicions; but this Great Britain had refused to Venezuela, and thus far had also denied to us.

Recreancy to a principle so fundamentally American as the Monroe Doctrine, on the part of those charged with the administration of our Government, was of course out of the question. Inasmuch, therefore, as all our efforts to avoid its assertion had miscarried, there was nothing left for us to do consistently with national honor but to take the place of Venezuela in the controversy, so far as that was necessary, in vindication of our American doctrine. Our mild and amiable proffers of good offices, and the hopes we indulged that at last they might be the means of securing to a weak sister republic peace and justice, and to ourselves immunity from sterner interposition, were not suited to the new emergency. In the advanced condition of the dispute, sympathy with Venezuela and solicitude for her distressed condition could no longer constitute the motive power of our conduct, but these were to give way to the duty and obligation of protecting our own national rights.

Mr. Gresham, who since the fourth day of March, 1893, had been our Secretary of State, died in the latter days of May, 1895. His love of justice, his sympathy with every cause that deserved sympathy, his fearless and disinterested patriotism, and his rare mental endowments, combined to make him a noble American and an able advocate of his country's honor. To such a man every phase of the Venezuelan boundary dispute strongly appealed; and he had been conscientiously diligent in acquainting himself with its history and in considering the contingencies that might arise in its future development. Though his death was most lamentable, I have always considered it a providential circumstance that the Government then had among its Cabinet officers an exceptionally strong and able man, in every way especially qualified to fill the vacant place, and thoroughly familiar with the pending controversy—which seemed every day to bring us closer to momentous duty and responsibility.

Mr. Olney was appointed Secretary of State early in June, 1895; and promptly thereafter, at the suggestion of the President, he began, with characteristic energy and vigor, to make preparation for the decisive step which it seemed should no longer be delayed.

The seriousness of the business we had in hand was fully understood, and the difficulty or impossibility of retracing the step we contemplated was thoroughly appreciated. The absolute necessity of certainty concerning the facts which should underlie our action was, of course, perfectly apparent. Whatever our beliefs or convictions might be, as derived from the examination we had thus far given the case, and however strongly we might be persuaded that Great Britain's pretensions could not be conceded consistently with our maintenance of the Monroe Doctrine, it would, nevertheless, have been manifestly improper and heedless on our part to find conclusively against Great Britain, before soliciting her again and in new circumstances to give us an opportunity to judge of the merits of her claims through the submission of them to arbitration.

It was determined, therefore, that a communication should be prepared for presentation to the British Government through our ambassador to England, detailing the progress and incidents of the controversy as we apprehended them, giving a thorough exposition of the origin of the Monroe Doctrine, and the reasons on which it was based, demonstrating our interest in the controversy because of its relation to that doctrine, and from our new standpoint and on our own account requesting Great Britain to join Venezuela in submitting to arbitration their contested claims to the entire territory in dispute.

This was accordingly done; and a despatch to this effect, dated July 20, 1895, was sent by Mr. Olney to her Majesty's Government through Mr. Bayard, our ambassador.

The Monroe Doctrine may be abandoned; we may forfeit it by taking our lot with nations that expand by following un-American ways; we may outgrow it, as we seem to be outgrowing other things we once valued; or it may forever stand as a guaranty of protection and safety in our enjoyment of free institutions; but in no event will this American principle ever be better defined, better defended, or more bravely asserted than was done by Mr. Olney in this despatch.

After referring to the various incidents of the controversy, and stating the conditions then existing, it was declared:

> The accuracy of the foregoing analysis of the existing status cannot, it is believed, be challenged. It shows that status to be such, that those charged with the interests of the United States are now forced to determine exactly what those interests are and what course of action they require. It compels them to decide to what extent, if any, the United States may and should intervene in a controversy between, and primarily concerning, only Great Britain and Venezuela, and to decide how far it is bound to see that the integrity of Venezuelan territory is not impaired by the pretensions of its powerful antagonist.

After an exhaustive explanation and vindication of the Monroe Doctrine, and after asserting that aggressions by Great Britain on Venezuelan soil would fall within its purview, the despatch proceeded as follows:

> While Venezuela charges such usurpation, Great Britain denies it; and the United States, until the merits are authoritatively ascertained, can take sides with neither. But while this is so,—while the United States may not, under existing circumstances at least, take upon itself to say which of the two parties is right and which is wrong,—it is certainly within its right to demand that the truth be ascertained. Being entitled to resent and resist any sequestration of Venezuelan soil by Great Britain, it is necessarily entitled to know whether such sequestration has occurred or is now going on.... It being clear, therefore, that the United States may legitimately insist upon the merits of the boundary question being determined, it is equally clear that there is but one feasible mode of determining them, viz., peaceful arbitration.

The demand of Great Britain that her right to a portion of the disputed territory should be acknowledged as a condition of her consent to arbitration as to the remainder, was thus characterized:

It is not perceived how such an attitude can be defended, nor how it is reconcilable with that love of justice and fair play so eminently characteristic of the English race. It in effect deprives Venezuela of her free agency and puts her under virtual duress. Territory acquired by reason of it will be as much wrested from her by the strong hand as if occupied by British troops or covered by British fleets.

The despatch, after directing the presentation to Lord Salisbury of the views it contained, concluded as follows:

They call for a definite decision upon the point whether Great Britain will consent or decline to submit the Venezuelan boundary question in its entirety to impartial arbitration. It is the earnest hope of the President that the conclusion will be on the side of arbitration, and that Great Britain will add one more to the conspicuous precedents she has already furnished in favor of that wise and just mode of settling international disputes. If he is to be disappointed in that hope, however,—a result not to be anticipated, and in his judgment calculated to greatly embarrass the future relations between this country and Great Britain,—it is his wish to be made acquainted with the fact at such early date as will enable him to lay the whole subject before Congress in his next annual message.

VI

The reply of Great Britain to this communication consisted of two despatches addressed by Lord Salisbury to the British ambassador at Washington for submission to our Government. Though dated the twenty-sixth day of November, 1895, these despatches were not presented to our State Department until a number of days after the assemblage of the Congress in the following month. In one of these communications Lord Salisbury, in dealing with the Monroe Doctrine and the right or propriety of our appeal to it in the pending controversy, declared: "The dangers which were apprehended by President Monroe have no relation to the state of things in which we live at the present day." He further declared:

But the circumstances with which President Monroe was dealing and those to which the present American Government is addressing itself have very few features in common. Great Britain is imposing no "system" upon

Venezuela and is not concerning herself in any way with the nature of the political institutions under which the Venezuelans may prefer to live. But the British Empire and the Republic of Venezuela are neighbors, and they have differed for some time past, and continue to differ, as to the line by which their dominions are separated. It is a controversy with which the United States have no apparent practical concern.... The disputed frontier of Venezuela has nothing to do with any of the questions dealt with by President Monroe.

His Lordship, in commenting upon our position as developed in Mr. Olney's despatch, defined it in these terms: "If any independent American state advances a demand for territory of which its neighbor claims to be the owner, and that neighbor is a colony of an European state, the United States have a right to insist that the European state shall submit the demand and its own impugned rights to arbitration."

I confess I should be greatly disappointed if I believed that the history I have attempted to give of this controversy did not easily and promptly suggest that this definition of our contention fails to take into account some of its most important and controlling features.

Speaking of arbitration as a method of terminating international differences, Lord Salisbury said:

It has proved itself valuable in many cases, but it is not free from defects which often operate as a serious drawback on its value. It is not always easy to find an arbitrator who is competent and who, at the same time, is wholly free from bias; and the task of insuring compliance with the award when it is made is not exempt from difficulty. It is a mode of settlement of which the value varies much according to the nature of the controversy to which it is applied and the character of the litigants who appeal to it. Whether in any particular case it is a suitable method of procedure is generally a delicate and difficult question. The only parties who are competent to decide that question are the two parties whose rival contentions are in issue. The claim of a third nation which is unaffected by the controversy to impose this particular procedure on either of the two others cannot be reasonably justified and has no foundation in the law of nations.

Immediately following this statement his Lordship again touched upon the Monroe Doctrine for the purpose of specifically disclaiming its acceptance by her Majesty's Government as a sound and valid principle. He says:

It must always be mentioned with respect, on account of the distinguished statesman to whom it is due and the great nation who have generally adopted it. But international law is founded on the general consent of nations; and no statesman, however eminent, and no nation, however powerful, are competent to insert into the code of international law a novel principle which was never recognized before, and which has not since been accepted by the Government of any other country. The United States have a right, like any other nation, to interpose in any controversy by which their own interests are affected; and they are the judge whether those interests are touched and in what measure they should be sustained. But their rights are in no way strengthened or extended by the fact that the controversy affects some territory which is called American.

In concluding this despatch Lord Salisbury declared that her Majesty's Government "fully concur with the view which President Monroe apparently entertained, that any disturbance of the existing territorial distribution in that hemisphere by any fresh acquisitions on the part of any European state would be a highly inexpedient change. But they are not prepared to admit that the recognition of that expediency is clothed with the sanction which belongs to a doctrine of international law. They are not prepared to admit that the interests of the United States are necessarily concerned in any frontier dispute which may arise between any two of the states who possess dominions in the Western Hemisphere; and still less can they accept the doctrine that the United States are entitled to claim that the process of arbitration shall be applied to any demand for the surrender of territory which one of those states may make against another."

The other despatch of Lord Salisbury, which accompanied the one upon which I have commented, was mainly devoted to a statement of facts and evidence on Great Britain's side in the boundary controversy; and in making such statement his Lordship in general terms designated the territory to which her Majesty's Government was entitled as being embraced within the lines of the most extreme claim which she had at any time presented. He added:

A portion of that claim, however, they have always been willing to waive altogether; in regard to another portion they have been and continue to be perfectly ready to submit the question of their title to arbitration. As regards the rest, that which lies within the so-called Schomburgk line, they do not consider that the rights of Great Britain are open to question. Even within that line they have on various occasions offered to Venezuela considerable concessions as a matter of friendship and conciliation and for the purpose of securing an amicable settlement of the dispute. If, as time has gone on, the concessions thus offered have been withdrawn, this has been the necessary consequence of the gradual spread over the country of British settlements, which Her Majesty's Government cannot in justice to the inhabitants offer to surrender to foreign rule.

In conclusion his Lordship asserts that his Government has

repeatedly expressed their readiness to submit to arbitration the conflicting claims of Great Britain and Venezuela to large tracts of territory which from their auriferous nature are known to be of almost untold value. But they cannot consent to entertain, or to submit to the arbitration of another power or of foreign jurists however eminent, claims based on the extravagant pretensions of Spanish officials in the last century and involving the transfer of large numbers of British subjects, who have for many years enjoyed the settled rule of a British colony, to a nation of different race and language, whose political system is subject to frequent disturbance, and whose institutions as yet too often afford very inadequate protection to life and property.

These despatches exhibit a refusal to admit such an interest in the controversy on our part as entitled us to insist upon an arbitration for the purpose of having the line between Great Britain and Venezuela established; a denial of such force or meaning to the Monroe Doctrine as made it worthy of the regard of Great Britain in the premises; and a fixed and continued determination on the part of her Majesty's Government to reject arbitration as to any territory included within the extended Schomburgk line. They further indicate that the existence of gold within the disputed territory had not been overlooked; and they distinctly put forward the colonization and settlement by English subjects in such territory, during more than half a century of dispute, as creating a claim to dominion and sovereignty, if not strong enough to override all question of right and title, at least so clear and indisputable as to be properly considered as above and beyond the contingencies of arbitration.

If we had been obliged to accept Lord Salisbury's estimate of the Monroe Doctrine, and his ideas of our interest, or rather want of interest, in the settlement of the boundary between Great Britain and Venezuela, his despatches would have certainly been very depressing. It would have been unpleasant for us to know that a doctrine which we had supposed for seventy years to be of great value and importance to us and our national safety was, after all, a mere plaything with which we might amuse ourselves; and that our efforts to enforce it were to be regarded by Great Britain and other European nations as meddlesome interferences with affairs in which we could have no legitimate concern.

The reply of the English Government to Mr. Olney's despatch, whatever else it accomplished, seemed absolutely to destroy any hope we might have entertained that, in our changed position in the controversy and upon our independent solicitation, arbitration might be conceded to us. Since, therefore, Great Britain was unwilling, on any consideration, to coöperate with Venezuela in setting on foot an investigation of their contested claim, and since prudence and care dictated that any further steps we might take should be proved to be as fully justified as was practicable in the circumstances, there seemed to be no better way open to us than to inaugurate a careful independent investigation of the merits of the controversy, on our own motion, with a view of determining as accurately as possible, for our own guidance, where the divisional line between the two countries should be located.

Mr. Olney's despatch and Lord Salisbury's reply were submitted to the Congress on the seventeenth day of December, 1895, accompanied by a message from the President.

In this message the President, after stating Lord Salisbury's positions touching the Monroe Doctrine, declared:

> Without attempting extended argument in reply to these positions, it may not be amiss to suggest that the doctrine upon which we stand is strong and sound, because its enforcement is important to our peace and safety as a nation, and is essential to the integrity of our free institutions and the tranquil maintenance of our distinctive form of government. It was intended to apply to every stage of our national life, and cannot become obsolete while our Republic endures. If the balance of power is justly a cause for jealous anxiety among the governments of the Old World and a subject for our absolute non-

interference, none the less is the observance of the Monroe Doctrine of vital concern to our people and their Government.

Speaking of the claim made by Lord Salisbury that this doctrine had no place in international law, it was said in the message: "The Monroe Doctrine finds its recognition in those principles of international law which are based upon the theory that every nation shall have its rights protected and its just claims enforced."

Referring to the request contained in Mr. Olney's despatch that the entire boundary controversy be submitted to arbitration, the following language was used:

It will be seen from the correspondence herewith submitted that this proposition has been declined by the British Government upon grounds which in the circumstances seem to me to be far from satisfactory. It is deeply disappointing that such an appeal, actuated by the most friendly feelings toward both nations directly concerned, addressed to the sense of justice and to the magnanimity of one of the great powers of the world, and touching its relations to one comparatively weak and small, should have produced no better results.

The course to be pursued by this Government in view of the present condition does not appear to admit of serious doubt. Having labored faithfully for many years to induce Great Britain to submit their dispute to impartial arbitration, and having been finally apprised of her refusal to do so, nothing remains but to accept the situation, to recognize its plain requirements, and deal with it accordingly. Great Britain's present proposition has never thus far been regarded as admissible by Venezuela, though any adjustment of the boundary which that country may deem for her advantage and may enter into of her own free will cannot, of course, be objected to by the United States. Assuming, however, that the attitude of Venezuela will remain unchanged, the dispute has reached such a stage as to make it now incumbent upon the United States to take measures to determine with sufficient certainty for its justification what is the true divisional line between the Republic of Venezuela and British Guiana. The inquiry to that end should, of course, be conducted carefully and judicially; and due weight should be given to all available evidence, records, and facts in support of the claims of both parties.

After recommending to the Congress an adequate appropriation to meet the expense of a commission which should make the suggested investigation and report thereon with the least possible delay, the President concluded his message as follows:

> When such report is made and accepted, it will, in my opinion, be the duty of the United States to resist by every means in its power, as a wilful aggression upon its rights and interests, the appropriation by Great Britain of any lands or the exercise of governmental jurisdiction over any territory which after investigation we have determined of right belongs to Venezuela.
>
> In making these recommendations I am fully alive to the responsibility incurred, and keenly realize all the consequences that may follow.
>
> I am, nevertheless, firm in my conviction that while it is a grievous thing to contemplate the two great English-speaking peoples of the world as being otherwise than friendly competitors in the onward march of civilization, and strenuous and worthy rivals in all the arts of peace, there is no calamity which a great nation can invite which equals that which follows a supine submission to wrong and injustice, and the consequent loss of national self-respect and honor, beneath which are shielded and defended a people's safety and greatness.

The recommendations contained in this message were acted upon with such promptness and unanimity that on the twenty-first day of December, 1895, four days after they were submitted, a law was passed by the Congress authorizing the President to appoint a commission "to investigate and report upon the true divisional line between the Republic of Venezuela and British Guiana," and making an ample appropriation to meet the expenses of its work.

On the first day of January, 1896, five of our most able and distinguished citizens were selected to constitute the commission; and they immediately entered upon their investigation. At the outset of their labors, and on the fifteenth day of January, 1896, the president of the commission suggested to Mr. Olney the expediency of calling the attention of the Governments of Great Britain and Venezuela to the appointment of the commission, adding: "It may be that they would see a way entirely consistent with their own sense of international propriety to give the Commission the aid that it is no doubt in their power to furnish in the way of documentary proof, historical narrative, unpublished archives, or the like." This suggestion, on its presentation to the Government of Great Britain, was met by a most courteous and willing offer to supply to our commission every means of information touching the subject of their investigation which was within the reach of the English authorities; and at all times during the labors of the commission this offer was cheerfully fulfilled.

In the meantime, and as early as February, 1896, the question of submitting the Venezuelan boundary dispute to mutual arbitration was again agitated between the United States and Great Britain.

Our ambassador to England, in a note to Lord Salisbury, dated February 27, 1896, after speaking of such arbitration as seeming to be "almost unanimously desired by both the United States and Great Britain," proposed, in pursuance of instructions from his Government, "an entrance forthwith upon negotiations at Washington to effect this purpose, and that Her Majesty's Ambassador at Washington should be empowered to discuss the question at that capital with the Secretary of State." He also requested that a definition should be given of "settlements" in the disputed territory which it was understood her Majesty's Government desired should be excluded from the proposed submission to arbitration.

Lord Salisbury, in his reply to this note, dated March 3, 1896, said:

> The communications which have already passed between Her Majesty's Government and that of the United States have made you acquainted with the desire of Her Majesty's Government to bring the difference between themselves and the Republic of Venezuela to an equitable settlement. They therefore readily concur in the suggestion that negotiations for this purpose should be opened at Washington without unnecessary delay. I have accordingly empowered Sir Julian Pauncefote to discuss the question either with the representative of Venezuela or with the Government of the United States acting as the friend of Venezuela.

With this transfer of treaty negotiations to Washington, Mr. Olney and Sir Julian Pauncefote, the ambassador of Great Britain to this country, industriously addressed themselves to the subject. The insistence of Great Britain that her title to the territory within the Schomburgk line should not be questioned, was no longer placed by her in the way of submitting the rights of the parties in the entire disputed territory to arbitration. She still insisted, however, that English settlers long in the occupancy of any of the territory in controversy, supposing it to be under British dominion, should have their rights scrupulously considered. Any difference of view that arose from this proposition was adjusted without serious difficulty, by agreeing that adverse holding or prescription during a period of fifty years should make a good title, and that the arbitrators might deem exclusive political control of a district, as well as actual settlement, sufficient to constitute adverse holding or to make title by prescription.

On the 10th of November, 1896, Mr. Olney addressed a note to the president of the commission which had been appointed to investigate the boundary question on behalf of our Government, in which he said: "The United States and Great Britain are in entire accord as to the provisions of a proposed treaty between Great Britain and Venezuela. The treaty is so eminently just and fair as respects both parties—so thoroughly protects the rights and claims of Venezuela—that I cannot conceive of its not being approved by the Venezuelan President and Congress. It is thoroughly approved by the counsel of Venezuela here and by the Venezuelan Minister at this Capital." In view of these conditions he suggested a suspension of the work of the commission.

The treaty was signed at Washington by the representatives of Great Britain and Venezuela on the second day of February, 1897. No part of the territory in dispute was reserved from the arbitration it created. It was distinctly made the duty of those appointed to carry out its provisions, "to determine the boundary-line between the Colony of British Guiana and the United States of Venezuela."

The fact must not be overlooked that, notwithstanding this treaty was promoted and negotiated by the officers of our Government, the parties to it were Great Britain and Venezuela. This was a fortunate circumstance, inasmuch as the work accomplished was thus saved from the risk of customary disfigurement at the hands of the United States Senate.

The arbitrators began their labors in the city of Paris in January, 1899, and made their award on the third day of October in the same year.

The line they determined upon as the boundary-line between the two countries begins in the coast at a point considerably south and east of the mouth of the Orinoco River, thus giving to Venezuela the absolute control of that important waterway, and awarding to her valuable territory near it. Running inland, the line is so located as to give to Venezuela quite a considerable section of territory within the Schomburgk line. This results not only in the utter denial of Great Britain's claim to any territory lying beyond the Schomburgk line, but also in the award to Venezuela of a part of the territory which for a long time England had claimed to be so clearly hers that she would not consent to submit it to arbitration.

Thus, we have made a laborious and patient journey through the incidents of a long dispute, to find at last a peaceful rest. As we look back over the road we have traversed, and view again the incidents we have passed on our way, some may be surprised that this controversy was so long chronic, and yet, in the end, yielded so easily to pronounced treatment. I know that occasionally some Americans of a certain sort, who were quite un-American when the difficulty was pending, have been very fond of lauding the extreme forbearance and kindness of England toward us in our so-called belligerent and ill-advised assertion of American principle. Those to whom this is a satisfaction are quite welcome to it.

My own surprise and disappointment have arisen more from the honest misunderstanding and the dishonest and insincere misrepresentation, on the part of many of our people, regarding the motives and purposes of the interference of the Government of the United States in this affair. Some conceited and doggedly mistaken critics have said that it was dreadful for us to invite war for the sake of a people unworthy of our consideration, and for the purpose of protecting their possession of land not worth possessing. It is certainly strange that any intelligent citizen, professing information on public affairs, could fail to see that when we aggressively interposed in this controversy it was because it was necessary in order to assert and vindicate a principle distinctively American, and in the maintenance of which the people and Government of the United States were profoundly concerned. It was because this principle was endangered, and because those charged with administrative responsibility would not abandon or neglect it, that our Government interposed to prevent any further colonization of American soil by a European nation. In these circumstances neither the character of the people claiming the soil as against Great Britain, nor the value of the lands in dispute, was of the least consequence to us; nor did it in the least concern us which of the two contestants had the best title to any part of the disputed territory, so long as England did not possess and colonize more than belonged to her—however much or however little that might be. But we needed proof of the limits of her rights in order to determine our duty in defense of our Monroe Doctrine; and we sought to obtain such proof, and to secure peace, through arbitration.

But those among us who most loudly reprehended and bewailed our vigorous assertion of the Monroe Doctrine were the timid ones who feared personal financial loss, or those engaged in speculation and stock-gambling, in buying much beyond their ability to pay, and generally in living by their wits. The patriotism of such people traverses exclusively the pocket nerve. They are willing to tolerate the Monroe Doctrine, or any other patriotic principle, so long as it does not interfere with their plans, and are just as willing to cast it off when it becomes troublesome.

But these things are as nothing when weighed against the sublime patriotism and devotion to their nation's honor exhibited by the great mass of our countrymen—the plain people of the land. Though, in case of the last extremity, the chances and suffering of conflict would have fallen to their lot, nothing blinded them to the manner in which the integrity of their country was involved. Not for a single moment did their Government know the lack of their strong and stalwart support.

I hope there are but few of our fellow-citizens who, in retrospect, do not now acknowledge the good that has come to our nation through this episode in our history. It has established the Monroe Doctrine on lasting foundations before the eyes of the world; it has given us a better place in the respect and consideration of the people of all nations, and especially of Great Britain; it has again confirmed our confidence in the overwhelming prevalence among our citizens of disinterested devotion to American honor; and last, but by no means least, it has taught us where to look in the ranks of our countrymen for the best patriotism.